2009

SO-AFY-334

Love, Mom

# 101 PEOPLE YOU WON'T MEET IN HEAVEN

To buy books in quantity for corporate use
or incentives, call **(800) 962–0973**
or e-mail **premiums@GlobePequot.com.**

Copyright © North America: The Globe Pequot Press

ALL RIGHTS RESERVED. No part of this book may be reproduced or transmitted in any form by any means,
electronic or mechanical, including photocopying and recording, or by any information storage and retrieval
system, except as may be expressly permitted in writing from the publisher. Requests for permission should be
addressed to The Lyons Press, Attn: Rights and Permissions Department, P.O. Box 480, Guilford, CT 06437.

First Lyons Press edition, 2007
The Lyons Press is an imprint of The Globe Pequot Press

10  9  8  7  6  5  4  3  2  1

Printed and bound in Hong Kong
Written by Michael Powell
Illustrations and photography, Scan Pix, Wikipedia

ISBN: 978-1-59921-105-3

Library of Congress Cataloging-in-Publication Data is available on file.

# 101 PEOPLE YOU WON'T MEET IN HEAVEN

## MICHAEL POWELL

THE LYONS PRESS
Guilford, Connecticut
An Imprint of The Globe Pequot Press

# CONTENTS

# INTRODUCTION

The twisted men and women who achieved the dubious honor of being included in this book are some of the most brutal and sadistic individuals who have walked the earth. They have committed unspeakable atrocities, from sticking friends and enemies on spikes, cannibalism, and torture, to human experimentation and genocide.

Some performed their crimes while the world passively observed, others while alarms sounded have eluded capture, and in one case at least, identification. Some are well known, others have silently passed through this world dedicating their lives to hate and cruelty, overshadowed by the more infamous icons of evil. Sometimes the quieter ones seem even more sinister because their actions often escape censure during their lifetime. Some are still at large and very much alive.

It is no surprise that most of the members of this hall of infamy are men. There are a handful of women, but seeing as it is men who have had most of the power throughout history, it is men who have abused this privilege, or sought to gain it by enacting their iniquitous misdeeds.

# IDI AMIN

- **BIRTH NAME:** Idi Awo-Ongo Angoo
- **TITLES:** "His Excellency President for Life, Field Marshal Al Hadji Doctor Idi Amin, VC, DSO, MC, Lord of All the Beasts of the Earth and Fishes of the Sea, and Conqueror of the British Empire in Africa in General and Uganda in Particular," "King of Scotland"
- **BIRTH:** c. 1924, Koboko, Uganda
- **DEATH:** August 16, 2003, heart attack

## WHO WAS HE?
He was the President of Uganda from 1971 to 1979.

## EARLY INFLUENCES
He was born into the small Kakwa tribe and grew up with his mother after his father abandoned him. After leaving school he joined the British army in the King's African Rifles in 1943, where he was described by his British superiors as "a splendid type, and a good rugby player, but virtually bone from the neck up." By 1954 he had reached

the rank of effendi (warrant officer), the highest rank possible for a black African in the British army. He was also the light heavyweight boxing champion of Uganda. After independence he became commander of the army in Milton Obote's government, and then in 1971 he seized power during a military coup, after learning that Obote was going to have him arrested for misappropriating army funds.

## WHAT DID HE DO THAT WAS SO WRONG?

His regime tortured thousands of members of rival tribes, the intelligentsia, and anyone who supported Obote. These killings were performed by death squads from the "State Research Bureau." He murdered the husbands and boyfriends of any women that he wanted to take for his own, and often kept their body parts in a fridge. He is also rumored to have been cannibalistic, though this has never been proven.

In August 1972 he gave the entire Ugandan Asian population ninety days to leave the country after getting the idea during a nocturnal vision. This led to the collapse of the country's economy, since many of them owned big businesses in Uganda.

In later years his behavior became increasingly paranoid and erratic. He granted himself many titles including "King of Scotland" and was a figure of ridicule throughout the world.

## BODY COUNT

His regime was responsible for the torture and murder of up to 500,000 Ugandans.

## FAMOUS QUOTES

"I myself consider myself the most powerful figure in the world."

"In any country there must be people who have to die. They are the sacrifices any nation has to make to achieve law and order."

"I ate them before they ate me."

# ATTILA THE HUN

- **BIRTH NAME:** Attila
- **TITLES:** "King of the Huns," "Scourge of God"
- **BIRTH:** 405
- **DEATH:** 453, burst artery

## WHO WAS HE?

He was the last and most powerful king of the Huns, who conquered an empire of well over a million square miles, stretching from Central Europe to the Black Sea and from the Danube River to the Baltic.

## EARLY INFLUENCES

Attila's father died when he was very young and the Huns were a migratory people, so from an early age Attila would have been accustomed to moving his tented house and possessions from place to place. Like all Huns he would have been able to ride a horse almost before he could walk, and he could wield a bow and arrow by the time he was five. When his uncle, King Ruga, sealed a peace treaty with the Roman Empire, young Attila was sent to live with the Romans in Ravenna as an insurance policy, where he received a good education, but grew to despise Roman decadence. When he was in his twenties he returned to his people, and while his brother Bleda became king, Attila created an army of ferocious sadists, and eventually murdered his brother to take the Hun throne in AD 445.

## WHAT DID HE DO THAT WAS SO WRONG?

He created an enormous fighting force by collaborating with other warlike tribes such as the Visigoths, Gepids, and Vandals. Then he rampaged through Europe raping, murdering, torturing, and dismembering all those who stood in his way. He razed scores of cities to the ground. On his way though Germany he proposed marriage to St. Ursula, the perpetual virgin. When she refused his advances he killed her and 11,000 of her pilgrim supporters.

The attack on the city of Naissus (Nis in Serbia) was so devastating that when Roman ambassadors passed through several years later, the smell of death was still so great that they camped outside the city, where they discovered hundreds of human bones.

After the Battle of Châlons, Attila's army tortured 200 young women by having them torn limb from limb tied to wild horses, or crushed under rolling wagons.

He is believed to have fathered over a hundred children with scores of wives, and is thought to have eaten his sons Erp and Eitil roasted in honey, served up to him by his wife.

## BODY COUNT

According to one chronicler, "There was so much killing and blood-letting that no one could number the dead." It is likely that deaths were in the hundreds of thousands.

## FAMOUS QUOTES

"Where I have passed, the grass will not grow again."

# GERTRUDE BANISZEWSKI

**■ BIRTH NAME:** Gertrude Van Fossan
**■ TITLES:** "The Torture Mother"
**■ BIRTH:** c. 1929
**■ DEATH:** 1990, lung cancer

## WHO WAS SHE?

She was an Indiana mother of seven children who took teenager Sylvia Likens into her house and then tortured and mutilated her for four months, and encouraged her children to join in, resulting in Sylvia's death.

## EARLY INFLUENCES

She was born into a family of six children, but little is known about her childhood, except that her father, to whom she was very close, died when she was eleven. She dropped out of school aged sixteen to enter into a physically abusive marriage. Baniszewski divorced in 1963, and brought up seven children on the poverty line and with failing health. In July 1965 she agreed to board two teenage sisters, Sylvia and Jenny Likens, whose mother was in prison.

## WHAT DID SHE DO THAT WAS SO WRONG?

Baniszewski's abuse of Sylvia began after her father failed to send money for her lodging. She beat her and made her eat her own vomit for being "greedy." A month later she violently attacked Sylvia, repeatedly kicking her, after overhearing her claim about a boy's overtures toward her. She encouraged her children to push Sylvia down the stairs, beat her, or use her as a kicking target for judo practice. On October 25, 1965, Sylvia was beaten to death with a chair, a paddle, and a broomstick.

Neighbors had witnessed some of the abuse and failed to inform the police, even when they heard the relentless banging of a shovel in the basement on the night of her death (it was Sylvia desperately calling for help); social services had visited the house but were persuaded that Sylvia had run away. Her sister Jenny had even smuggled a letter to her elder sister Diana, detailing the abuse, but she assumed that Jenny was making it up.

Baniszewski spent eighteen years in prison and was paroled on December 4, 1985. She changed her name and moved to Iowa where she died five years later.

## BODY COUNT

Baniszewski tortured and killed Sylvia Likens and was responsible for destroying the lives of Jenny Likens and her own children. Ricky Hobbs chain smoked himself to death from lung cancer, aged twenty-one, after the enormity of his own involvement had sunk in.

## FAMOUS QUOTES

"I'm not sure what role I had in it . . . because I was on drugs. I never really knew her . . . I take full responsibility for whatever happened to Sylvia."

# VELMA BARFIELD

- **BIRTH NAME:** Velma Margie Bullard
- **TITLES:** "Serial Killer"
- **BIRTH:** October 23, 1932, South Carolina, USA
- **DEATH:** November 2, 1984, lethal injection (execution)

## WHO WAS SHE?

She was a serial killer who poisoned several victims, including her mother, and she was the first woman in the United States to be executed since 1962.

## EARLY INFLUENCES

She was the second oldest child of nine, born to a tobacco and cotton farmer. Her father was very strict and regular beatings were the norm; later in life she accused him of sexual abuse. Despite being bright, her grades were low and she was unpopular at school because of her poor background and she became involved in petty theft. She left home at seventeen to marry her boyfriend, Thomas Burke, and by the early fifties had two children. For the first time in her life she was happy and became a model parent.

## WHAT DID SHE DO THAT WAS SO WRONG?

Her problems began after she had a hysterectomy in 1965, which left her suffering severe mood swings and depression. The same year her husband suffered a concussion in a car accident and started drinking heavily to deal with the severe headaches. As tension increased at home Velma became addicted to Valium and other tranquilizers. After her husband died in a house fire she married Jenning Barfield in 1970—her first victim, whom she poisoned with arsenic (her poison of choice), then went to live with her parents.

After her father died of lung cancer she poisoned her mother over the Christmas holiday of 1974. The following year she was sent to prison for six months for writing bad checks. After her release she got a job as a caregiver to an elderly couple, but by February 1977 she had poisoned both of them. She poisoned her next charge, eighty-year-old John Henry Lee, and moved in with her fifty-six-year-old boyfriend, Stuart Taylor, who became her final victim.

She was turned in by her sister. Velma confessed first to her son, and later the police.

## BODY COUNT
She poisoned six people, including her own mother.

## FAMOUS QUOTES
"I want to say that I am sorry for all the hurt that I have caused. I know that everybody has gone through a lot of pain—all the families connected—and I am sorry, and I want to thank everybody who has been supporting me all these six years. I want to thank my family for standing with me through all this and my attorneys and all the support to me, everybody, the people with the prison department. I appreciate everything—their kindness and everything that they have shown me during these six years."

"When I go into that chamber at 2.00 A.M. it's my gateway to heaven."

# BASIL II

- **BIRTH NAME:** Prince Basil
- **TITLES:** "The Bulgar-slayer"
- **BIRTH:** 958, Macedonia
- **DEATH:** December 15, 1025

## WHO WAS HE?

He was a ruthless Byzantine emperor who led the Byzantine Empire to its greatest heights in nearly five centuries.

## EARLY INFLUENCES

Basil was the son of Romanus II and Theophano, and with his brother was crowned co-emperor of the Byzantine Empire when he was two years old, although he was too young to reign and only took effective power when he was eighteen. He was more interested in military and carnal pursuits than intellectual interests, although he was a good administrator and a commanding orator. He distinguished himself as an excellent horseman and brave soldier.

During his adolescence and his early twenties he led a profligate existence, with regular debauched orgies and banquets. Then he set his sights on expanding his empire.

## WHAT DID HE DO THAT WAS SO WRONG?

In 1014 Basil was victorious in the thirty-year war against the Bulgars, defeating them at the decisive Battle of Kledion in the upper valley of the Struma River, after which he took 14,000 prisoners of war. He didn't want to kill them, but he knew that if he let them go they would still pose a threat. He decided upon a gruesome compromise: he ordered his soldiers to gouge out the eyes of every single prisoner, but to leave every hundredth man with one eye intact, so that they could lead the rest of their comrades home.

Basil's soldiers used red hot pokers and daggers to carry out his orders, and then the blinded men made the agonizing trek back to Tsar Samuel's castle of Ochrid, in modern Macedonia. Many men died during the journey, and the Tsar is reported to have died of a stroke when he saw how his loyal troops had been mutilated.

Undaunted by his cruelty, Basil used the same tactic two years later, during a military campaign in Macedonia, blinding every Bulgarian his army captured, including women and children.

## BODY COUNT

The number of soldiers who died during his military campaigns is unknown, but his greatest legacy was the blinding of 14,000 prisoners.

# ELIZABETH BÁTHORY

- **BIRTH NAME:** Erzsébet Báthory
- **TITLES:** "Bloody Lady of Čachtice," "The Blood Countess"
- **BIRTH:** August 7, 1560, Nyírbátor, Hungary
- **DEATH:** August 21, 1614

## WHO WAS SHE?

She was a Hungarian countess considered to be the world's most prolific mass murderer.

## EARLY INFLUENCES

The noble Báthory family was descended from the Hun Gutkeled clan which ruled large areas of east central Europe since the thirteenth century. Elizabeth's uncle had been King of Poland.

Elizabeth grew up in Ecsed Castle, but after becoming engaged at age eleven to a commander of the Hungarian army, she moved to his castle in Sarvar and married him four years later. Her wedding gift was Čachtice Castle and seventeen nearby villages. She bore him six children, two of which died at an early age. Her husband died in 1602. By then she had already been killing local peasant women for twenty years.

## WHAT DID SHE DO THAT WAS SO WRONG?

She and her four accomplices brought young peasant women to the castle, often on the pretext of offering them work, and subjected them to horrific tortures and murder, including freezing and starving victims to death, prolonged beating, and mutilation with a red-hot poker.

One of her cruelest torture weapons belonged to her husband, and was used to torture prisoners of war. It was an articulated claw-like device made out of silver that could be attached to the end of a whip, but it ripped flesh so effectively that her husband had stopped using it.

An enduring myth says that her best feature was her creamy white complexion and that she attempted to preserve her youthful appearance by bathing in a bath full of the blood of young virgins. She also bit pieces of flesh off her victims in blood frenzy, and had other victims smeared with honey and then chained in the woods to be devoured by wild animals.

In 1609, after deciding that she needed more noble blood for her bath, she established a finishing school at her castle, offering to take 25 girls at a time from good proper families, and to complete their educations. Now that she was killing girls from better stock, her actions came to the attention of King Mathias II, and she was arrested in December 1610, and imprisoned in her castle until her death four years later.

## BODY COUNT

She tortured and killed between 600 and 1,000 girls and young women.

## FAMOUS QUOTES

"More! More still! Harder still!"

# FULGENCIO BATISTA Y ZALVÍDAR

- **BIRTH NAME:** Fulgencio Batista y Zalvídar
- **TITLES:** President of Cuba
- **BIRTH:** January 16, 1901, Banes, Cuba
- **DEATH:** August 6, 1973, heart attack

## WHO WAS HE?

He was the de facto military leader of Cuba from 1933 to 1940 and the President of Cuba from 1940 to 1944 and 1952 to 1959.

## EARLY INFLUENCES

He was the son of impoverished peasant laborers and Cuban independence fighters Belisario Batista and Carmela Zaldívar. He was self-educated and joined the army in 1921. In 1933 he was one of the leaders of the "Sergeants' Revolt" which replaced the Provisional Government of Carlos Manuel de Céspedes. Ramón Grau was made president and Batista became the Army Chief of Staff and effectively controlled the country over a succession of puppet presidents.

## WHAT DID HE DO THAT WAS SO WRONG?

As head of the military Batista violently suppressed all opposition, and crushed several attempted revolts, executing those who had surrendered.

In October, 1940, Batista was elected President of Cuba and began a huge public works program and greatly expanded the economy. With help from the Italian Mafia he turned Cuba into a sex-and-gambling resort island for the United States, while the bulk of the people remained in great poverty. Havana became known as the "Latin Las Vegas" and Batista and his friends became rich from numerous back handers from organized crime.

At the end of his first term Batista retired to Florida a multi-millionaire. He returned to Cuba in 1952 and took power again in a bloodless coup, then suppressed opposition even more violently than before and embezzled huge sums of money from the public coffers.

This widespread corruption led to the rise of an anti-government guerrilla movement led by Fidel Castro. In an attempt to hunt down supporters of Castro thousands of innocent people were tortured and killed. Any who were suspected of being pro-Castro, including children, were publicly executed and left hanging in the streets as a warning to others.

## BODY COUNT

Batista's regime was responsible for the deaths of thousands of Cubans. Many thousands more were tortured and forced into exile.

## FAMOUS QUOTES

"No one can now say Colonel Batista interferes with public powers... If my election is bad for Cuba then I hope I am not elected."

"I give Castro a year. No longer."

# PAUL BERNARDO & KARLA HOMOLKA

- **BIRTH NAME:** Paul Bernardo
- **TITLES:** "Scarborough Rapist"
- **BIRTH:** August 1964, Scarborough, Canada
- **DEATH:** still alive

- **BIRTH NAME:** Karla Homolka
- **BIRTH:** May 4, 1970, Port Credit, Canada
- **DEATH:** still alive

## WHO ARE THEY?

They were a Canadian married couple who abducted, drugged, raped, tortured, videoed, and killed their victims during the early nineties.

## EARLY INFLUENCES

Karla was the eldest of three sisters in a normal middle-class family. She grew up in Ontario and as a teenager worked part-time in a pet store. In October 1987 this job took her to a convention in Toronto, where she met Paul Bernardo. After graduating from high school she worked as a veterinary assistant.

Paul's father was a pedophile who was convicted of abusing Paul's sister, and was physically abusive to his mother. When he was sixteen Paul's mother told him that he was the product of an adulterous affair. From then on he despised her, and already hated his "father" for his sexual depravity. Until then Paul had been a popular and charming teenager, a good looking, caring and attentive boyfriend with many girls interested in him. After his mother's revelation his behavior changed.

## WHAT DID THEY DO THAT WAS SO WRONG?

In his early twenties Paul began to beat up and rape the women he dated. When he met Karla Homolka they quickly became sexually obsessed with each other and got engaged. By this time Paul was a serial rapist (known as the "Scarborough Rapist"), grabbing women as they got off buses, raping and sodomizimg them. When Karla learned about the rapes she encouraged them and videoed some of them.

Karla was prepared to do anything sexually to satisfy and keep her man, so when Paul demanded that she let him take her sister Tammy's virginity (as pay back for the fact that Karla was not a virgin when they met) she readily agreed. On December 23, 1990, at her family home with her parents upstairs asleep in bed, Karla drugged her sister with alcohol laced with a sedative, and used a rag soaked in an anesthetic she used at work to make her sister unconscious. The rape went awry, however, because the sister threw up and died from vomit inhalation. Her death was ruled an accident. Shortly afterwards Karla procured another fifteen-year-old girl and drugged her so that Paul could take her virginity. It was her wedding gift to him.

On June 14, 1991, Paul abducted fourteen-year-old Leslie Mahaffy, who had been shut out of her family house for coming home late. After she died during rough sex play, which was vidotaped, they cut up her body, buried the parts in concrete blocks, and dumped them in Lake Gibson. The remains were discovered the same day the couple got married.

On April 16, 1992, Karla lured another teenager, Kristen French, into their car; they abducted and eventually killed her.

In the summer of 1992 Karla filed assault charges against Paul and went to live in a refuge. She later confessed to police that Paul was a serial rapist and murderer. She plea bargained and spent twelve years in prison (she was released in July 2005); Paul is serving life without the possibility of parole.

In 1990 the police had interviewed Paul about the Scarborough rapes, and had taken blood samples. It was only in February of 1993 that tests were followed up, showing that he was the rapist. Had the laboratory and police processed these samples earlier, several rapes and murders could have been prevented.

## BODY COUNT

Paul is believed to have committed at least fourteen rapes, including one while the couple were on their honeymoon in Hawaii. He was found guilty on two counts of first-degree murder, two counts of aggravated assault, and kidnapping charges, but he has been linked with the murder of another fourteen-year-old in November 1991.

## FAMOUS QUOTES

"Don't make me mad. Don't make me hurt you . . . You're a f--king piece of shit. But I like you." (Video transcript of the torture of Kristen French)

# KENNETH BIANCHI & ANGELO BUONO

- **BIRTH NAME:** Kenneth Bianchi
- **TITLES:** "Hillside Strangler"
- **BIRTH:** May 22, 1951, Rochester, USA
- **DEATH:** still alive

**BIRTH NAME:** Angelo Buono
**TITLES:** "Hillside Strangler"
**BIRTH:** October 5, 1934, Rochester, USA
**DEATH:** September 21, 2002, heart attack

## WHO WERE THEY?

They were cousins who became known as the "Hillside Stranglers" for kidnapping, raping, torturing, and murdering girls and women during the late seventies in the hills above Los Angeles.

## EARLY INFLUENCES

Bianchi's mother was an alcoholic prostitute who gave him up for adoption at birth. From an early age he had a dysfunctional attitude towards women and was labeled a "compulsive liar." He married in 1971 but it only lasted eight months. He then studied police science and psychology at community college and dropped out, and became a security guard who stole from the premises he was supposed to protect.

Buono's parents divorced when he was young. In his early teens he began stealing cars and raping girls, and was sent to a reformatory for grand theft auto. He idolized the sex offender Caryl Chessman, the "red light rapist" who used to pose as a cop by shining a red light into cars. He had several wives and children, and sexually and physically assaulted all of them.

## WHAT DID THEY DO THAT WAS SO WRONG?

Together they began pimping young women that they met, keeping them as virtual prisoners. Then in October 1977 they began killing them, too. They subjected their victims to brutal rapes and torture before killing them by strangulation.

Two of their victims were schoolgirls abducted on their way home from school. Five of the murders happened around Thanksgiving, but the killers stopped during the holiday, and resumed killing after the festivities.

They asphyxiated one of their victims by covering her head with a bag and running a pipe into it from the stove. Many of the bodies were dumped in the hills above Los Angeles, hence the nickname "Hillside Stranglers."

They stopped the daughter of the actor Peter Lorre, intending to abduct her but changed their mind after discovering who here famous father was. She only realized her narrow escape after they were brought to trial.

## BODY COUNT

They raped and murdered ten children and young women between October 1977 and February 1978.

## FAMOUS QUOTES

"We dumped the body off and that was it. Nothing to it."

# JEAN-BÉDEL BOKASSA

**BIRTH NAME:** Jean-Bédel Bokassa

**TITLES:** "Emperor Bokassa I," "Emperor of Central Africa by the will of the Central African people, united within the national political party, the MESAN"

**BIRTH:** February 22, 1921, Bobangi, French Equatorial Africa (now Central African Republic)

**DEATH:** November 3, 1996, heart attack

## WHO WAS HE?

He was the military ruler from January 1, 1966, of the Central African Republic and from December 4, 1976, sole emperor of the Central African Empire until his overthrow on September 20, 1979.

## EARLY INFLUENCES

He was born into the M'Baka tribe. His father was the village chief, who was caned to death by a French administrator when Bokassa was six, and his mother committed suicide the following week. He was educated in Catholic mission schools then joined the French colonial army in 1939 and was awarded the Legion d'honneur and the Croix de guerre. In 1960 French Equatorial Africa became independent and was renamed the Central African Republic, led by his cousin, President David Dacko. Dacko made Bokassa chief of staff of the military, but on January 1, 1966, Bokassa overthrew him in a coup, and six years later declared himself president for life.

## WHAT DID HE DO THAT WAS SO WRONG?

He brutally suppressed crime and dissent. He introduced a system of punishment whereby a thief would have an ear cut off for the first two offences, and then a hand for the third.

In 1977 after declaring the republic a monarchy he crowned himself "emperor" in a Napoleonic ceremony that cost $22 million—almost one third of the country's yearly budget. He embezzled millions of dollars and lived in luxury, sleeping on a gold bed surrounded by jewels. He once had 100 school children massacred because they refused to wear the expensive school uniform required by law (and manufactured by one of his factories).

In September 1979 French paratroopers removed him from power and he fled to France. He returned in 1986 and was charged with embezzlement, murder, and cannibalism and although he was sentenced to solitary confinement for life, he was released after six years and died three years later. Towards the end of his life he declared himself to be the thirteenth Apostle and claimed to have secret meetings with the Pope. A fanatical stamp collector, another of his self-proclaimed monikers was "Grand Master of the International Brotherhood of Knights Collectors of Postage Stamps."

## BODY COUNT

He was found guilty of the murder of 100 school children, but hundreds of others were tortured and died under his regime.

## FAMOUS QUOTES

"The French Government pays for everything in our country. We ask the French for money. We get it, and then we waste it."

# IAN BRADY & MYRA HINDLEY

- **BIRTH NAME:** Ian Stewart
- **TITLES:** "The Moors Murderer"
- **BIRTH:** January 2, 1938, Glasgow, UK
- **DEATH:** still alive

- **BIRTH NAME:** Myra Hindley
- **TITLES:** "The Moors Murderer"
- **BIRTH:** July 23, 1942, Manchester, UK
- **DEATH:** November 15, 2002, heart attac

## WHO WERE THEY?

They were lovers known as "The Moors Murderers," responsible for the rape, torture, and murder of five children between 1963 and 1965 on and around Saddleworth Moor near Manchester, UK.

## EARLY INFLUENCES

Ian Brady's mother was single parent; to avoid the stigma of him being illegitimate she gave him to the nearby Sloane family to be raised. He was bright and handsome, but lazy, prone to violent rages and unpopular with local children. He also enjoyed bullying smaller children and torturing animals and became fascinated with all things Nazi. In his adolescence he worked as a butcher's assistant, and spent time in a borstal for petty theft. After his release he became a stock clerk at Millwards Merchandisers, where he met Myra Hindley.

Myra Hindley was raised by her grandmother, and was allegedly beaten by her alcoholic father. When she was fifteen she was deeply traumatized when one of her close friends drowned in a reservoir. She left school and was briefly engaged before becoming a typist at Millwards, where she became infatuated with Ian Brady. A year later they started dating and he began grooming her as his moll.

## WHAT DID THEY DO THAT WAS SO WRONG?

They abducted their first victim, sixteen-year-old Pauline Reade, on July 12, 1963, drove her to Saddleworth Moor, where Brady smashed her head with a shovel, raped her, slit her throat, and buried her in a shallow grave.

The next victim, twelve-year-old John Kilbride, was sexually assaulted, had his throat slit, and was then strangled with a shoelace and buried.

The following summer on June 16, 1964, they gave twelve-year-old Keith Bennett a lift, then drove him to the Moor where Brady sexually assaulted him, strangled him, and buried the body, which has never been found.

The fourth victim, ten-year-old Lesley Ann Downey, was abducted from a fairground on the day after Christmas in 1964 and taken back to Brady's home, where she was tortured, raped, and made to pose for obscene photographs. The couple made a sixteen-minute audio tape of her ordeal, before Hindley (according to Brady) strangled her.

The final victim, seventeen-year-old Edward Evans, was invited back to Brady's house on October 6, 1965, where Brady killed him with an axe, in front of Myra's brother-in-law, David Smith. Fearing for his life, Smith helped Brady carry the body upstairs, then went to the police and the couple were arrested.

## BODY COUNT
They tortured, raped, and killed five children over a two-year period.

## FAMOUS QUOTES
"I reached the stage where, whatever came to mind, get out and do it. I led the life that other people could only think about." (Ian Brady)

"It's done. It's the messiest yet. It normally only takes one blow." (Ian Brady)

# MARTIN BRYANT

- **BIRTH NAME:** Martin John Bryant
- **TITLES:** "Stupid Marty"
- **BIRTH:** May 7, 1967, Tasmania, Australia
- **DEATH:** still alive

## WHO IS HE?

He is a spree killer who was responsible for the Port Arthur Massacre in Tasmania in 1996.

## EARLY INFLUENCES

In his childhood Bryant's IQ was measured at only 66, which indicated mental disability. He was an isolated and disruptive child, unusually detached from reality and prone to violent outbursts. He was also bullied by the other children.

Bryant's father was found drowned with his son's diving belt around his neck. Although the verdict was suicide, Bryant's subsequent behavior and his apparent unconcern about his father's death, lends weight to the possibility that this was his first murder. Later he befriended a woman who died in a traffic accident, bequeathing him more than half a million dollars. He then traveled extensively, but became increasingly frustrated by his social isolation. He was obsessed with violent movies (especially the trilogy *Child's Play*), and collecting teddy bears.

## WHAT DID HE DO THAT WAS SO WRONG?

On Sunday April 28, 1996, he ate a meal at the Broad Arrow Café at the Port Arthur Historic Site on the island of Tasmania. After making a comment about the number of Japanese and white tourists, he took a self-loading AR-15 rifle and an SKS assault rifle out of his blue sports bag and started shooting. In just ninety seconds he killed twenty diners and wounded fifteen, then walked outside the café and killed a bus driver, followed by a woman and her two daughters, aged three and five. He also hunted down and shot at point blank range a five-year-old girl who hid behind a tree, after Bryant had shot her mother. At first some of the crowd thought that he was staging a harmless historical re-enactment.

Still shooting he made his way back to his car and drove to a gas station where he carjacked a couple. He shot the woman, and locked the man in the trunk. Then he drove to the Seascape Cottage guesthouse about 4 miles away, where he had earlier killed the two owners. He held the man hostage for sixteen hours, before setting fire to the cottage. He accidentally set himself alight and ran outside where he was arrested and taken to hospital with severe burns.

He is currently serving thirty-five life sentences in Hobart's Risdon Prison.

## BODY COUNT
He killed thirty-five people and wounded thirty-seven others; his victims ranged in age from three to seventy-two.

## FAMOUS QUOTES

"I'll do something that will make everyone remember me."

"I wish I'd had a few more friends. But I didn't have a great deal of friends at school so it made things difficult."

"I've got something important to do tomorrow."

# TED BUNDY

- **BIRTH NAME:** Theodore Robert Bundy
- **TITLES:** "Serial Killer"
- **BIRTH:** November 24, 1946, Burlington, Vermont, USA
- **DEATH:** January 24, 1989, electrocution (executed)

## WHO WAS HE?

He was an American serial killer and rapist who murdered scores of young women across the United States between 1974 and 1978.

## EARLY INFLUENCES

For the first nine years of his life he lived with his paternal grandfather, whom some family members claim was mentally unstable and violent. Also, to avoid the stigma of being born illegitimate, it is likely that Bundy grew up believing that his mother was his "sister."

He was a good student, but was shy and introverted, and had no natural sense of how to interact with people: "I didn't know what underlay social interactions." In his adolescence he became a shoplifter, voyeur, and window-peeper, and became obsessed with pornography.

## WHAT DID HE DO THAT WAS SO WRONG?

He is considered by some to be the prototypical serial killer. His preferred victim resembled a woman called Stephanie Brooks, his only serious relationship, which ended bitterly: young, white, and with long dark hair parted in the middle. He used his good looks and charm to get women to trust him, then brutally raped and murdered them. He often pretended to need help lifting something to his car (placing his arm in a sling) or posed as a cop.

It is possible that he began killing as early as fifteen (an eight-year-old girl disappeared from Bundy's neighborhood at that time), but his earliest confirmed murders took place in 1974, when he was twenty-seven. His first confirmed victim, eighteen-year-old student Karen Sparks, survived his assault, but was left with permanent brain damage and deafness. Over the next four years he raped and murdered his way across the country until his arrest on August 16, 1975. Some of his victims were beaten beyond recognition.

## BODY COUNT

He confessed to thirty murders, and has been linked to six others, but comments by Bundy have hinted that he killed many more, possibly as many as 136.

## FAMOUS QUOTES

"There was no physical abuse or fighting in the home. . . I led a normal life."

"I haven't blocked out the past. I wouldn't trade the person I am, or what I've done—or the people I've known—for anything. So I do think about it. And at times it's a rather mellow trip to lay back and remember."

"You are going to kill me, and that will protect society from me. But out there are many, many more people who are addicted to pornography, and you are doing nothing about that."

# CALIGULA

- **BIRTH NAME:** Gaius Caesar Augustus Germanicus
- **TITLES:** "Little Boot," "Emperor of Rome"
- **BIRTH:** August 31, 12, Tibur, Italy
- **DEATH:** January 24, 41, assassination

## WHO WAS HE?

He was the third Roman Emperor and was renowned for his unconventional behavior, extreme profligacy, and cruelty.

## EARLY INFLUENCES

He was brought up in the military camps of his father where the soldiers nicknamed him "Little Boot" because of his footwear. When he was seven his father died and following the execution of his mother and two brothers by Emperor Tiberius, Caligula grew up with the emperor on Capri. He married a noble woman, who died in childbirth, then had an affair with the wife of the commander of the Praetorian Guard, while at the same time becoming one of his most trusted companions.

## WHAT DID HE DO THAT WAS SO WRONG?

In his mid-twenties he murdered the unpopular Tiberius to become Emperor, but seven months later he fell ill with a fever which affected his brain and his behavior quickly deteriorated. He emptied the public coffers with his wild partying, and then staged treason trials to condemn innocent landowners to death so that their property could be forfeited to the state. He forced others to make him their sole beneficiary, before having them killed.

During public games, he had the disabled and the infirm fed to the lions, and had random members of the audience thrown into the arena to make up the numbers. He had one of the gladiator's managers flogged with a heavy chain for days on end, and only allowed him to be killed when the smell of his infected brain matter offended his nostrils.

He made parents watch the execution of their own children; he closed the public granaries so that his people would starve; he had one senator dismembered and the pieces dragged around the streets of Rome; and paraded a thief at a party with his amputated hands tied around his neck. He had a poet burned alive in public because he took offence at one of his verses; he committed incest with his sister; set up a brothel in his palace; and forced people into prostitution.

## BODY COUNT

He killed, raped, tortured, robbed, and abused thousands of his subjects. It is little wonder that he was stabbed by his own bodyguards.

## FAMOUS QUOTES

"Let them hate me, so they but fear me."

"Would that the Roman people had a single neck [to cut off their head]."

"Strike so that he may feel that he is dying."

# AL CAPONE

- **BIRTH NAME:** Alphonsus Capone
- **TITLES:** "Scarface," "The Big Fellow"
- **BIRTH:** January 17, 1899, Brooklyn, New York, USA
- **DEATH:** January 25, 1947, cardiac arrest

## WHO WAS HE?

He was an infamous Italian-American gangster in the 1920s and 1930s, Chicago's most notorious crime figure.

## EARLY INFLUENCES

He grew up in a tough Brooklyn neighborhood and was a gang member even as a child. He was bright, but left school at age fourteen. Some of his early jobs were in a candy store and a book bindery, until he joined the Five Points Gang and began working as a bouncer and bartender at the Harvard Inn, run by the gangster Frankie Yale. It was here that he received the facial scars that earned him the nickname "Scarface."

## WHAT DID HE DO THAT WAS SO WRONG?

Early in his career he murdered two men in New York, but was never tried: in keeping with gangland protocol, no one would testify against him. After he hospitalized a rival gang member, Yale sent him to Chicago where he worked for John Torrio in his bootlegging business, quickly rising to be his second in command. Torrio eventually handed the empire to Capone, which he developed during the twenties for a reported turnover of $100 million a year.

He was very efficient at dispatching his enemies and rivals, but he always had an alibi, so could never be brought to justice. The most famous of his contract killings was the St. Valentine's Day Massacre, on February 14, 1929, when seven members of the rival bootlegger George "Bugs" Moran's gang were gunned down in a garage. Capone was in Florida.

He was arrested several times, once for killing three people in 1926, but as usual there was insufficient evidence to convict him. He was finally successfully brought to trial for tax evasion, after the 1927 Sullivan Ruling claimed that illegal profits were in fact taxable. When a cash receipts ledger was discovered linking Capone to illegal gambling profits, tax lawyers were able to indict Capone in 1931 for tax evasion for the years 1925–29 and for failing to file tax returns. He was found guilty and sentenced to ten years in federal prison and one year in the county jail. He was sent to Atlanta prison, and then Alcatraz, where he became the model prisoner.

## BODY COUNT

Capone ordered dozens of deaths and even killed with his own hands.

## FAMOUS QUOTES

"You can go a long way with a smile. You can go a lot farther with a smile and a gun."

"When I sell liquor, it's called bootlegging; when my patrons serve it on Lake Shore Drive, it's called hospitality."

"I am like any other man. All I do is supply a demand."

# NICOLAE CEAUSESCU

- **BIRTH NAME:** Nicolae Ceausescu
- **TITLES:** "The Conducator," "Major General President of Romania"
- **BIRTH:** January 26, 1918, Scornicesti, Romania
- **DEATH:** December 25, 1989, shot (executed)

## WHO WAS HE?

He was the leader of Communist Romania from 1965 until shortly before his execution.

## EARLY INFLUENCES

The son of a peasant, at the age of eleven he moved to Bucharest to become a shoemaker's apprentice. At age fifteen he joined the then-illegal Communist Party of Romania and as a consequence was imprisoned six times. He worked his way up through the party to become secretary of the Union of Communist Youth. When the Communists took power he first became the minister of agriculture then deputy minister of the armed forces, and finally a full member of the Politburo in 1954. In March 1965, he became first secretary of the ruling Romanian Workers' Party and renamed the country the Socialist Republic of Romania.

## WHAT DID HE DO THAT WAS SO WRONG?

Impressed by the personality cult surrounding Mao Zedong and Kim Il Sung following a visit to China and North Korea in 1971, he set up his own. He challenged the supremacy of the Soviet Union, which made him a "friend" to the West which sent him millions in aid. He wasted the money on misguided public reform projects, such as bulldozing Romanian villages and moving people into huge hi-rise residential blocks. He beefed up the securitate (secret service) which systematically exterminated opponents of the regime, and sent dissidents to special camps to be worked to death. He built himself a string of palaces, including the People's Palace in Bucharest, which is the world's second largest building after the Pentagon. More than 7,000 buildings were demolished to make way for this expensive monstrosity, many of them historic, churches, schools, even hospitals.

The regime banned abortion and contraception, and taxed childless couples heavily. This caused population growth, which increased poverty causing many children to be abandoned and sent to state run orphanages in appalling conditions. In the late 1980s there was a rampant AIDS epidemic, caused by the state's refusal to acknowledge the problem, or even allow people to be tested for HIV.

After all this reckless spending, in the 1980s Ceausescu instituted an austerity program to pay back all the state debt, while he continued to live in obscene luxury (he wore a new suit every day during his twenty-five-year reign). He ordered the export of almost all the country's agricultural produce. This repayment policy left his people starving and lacking the most basic of amenities and supplies.

## BODY COUNT

He caused thousands of deaths per year during the 1980s from deprivations caused by the unnecessary austerity program. Tens of thousands of lives were ruined by his regime.

## FAMOUS QUOTES

"No, we had no palaces. The palaces belong to the people."

# RICHARD CHASE

- **BIRTH NAME:** Richard Trenton Chase
- **TITLES:** "The Vampire of Sacramento," "Dracula"
- **BIRTH:** May 23, 1950, Sacramento, USA
- **DEATH:** December 26, 1980, overdose (suicide)

## WHO WAS HE?

He was a schizophrenic mass murderer who killed six people, mutilated their bodies, ate their body organs, and drank their blood.

## EARLY INFLUENCES

He grew up in an abusive household and was beaten often by his father. As he grew older he enjoyed harming, mutilating, and killing small animals and starting fires. In his adolescence he developed a serious alcohol and drug problem.

In January 1978 he was institutionalized for paranoid schizophrenia, after complaining that his head kept changing shape and that someone had stolen his pulmonary artery. He was brought under control with medication but after his release he stopped taking it and his delusions returned. While in hospital the nursing staff nicknamed him "Dracula."

## WHAT DID HE DO THAT WAS SO WRONG?

He became convinced that his blood was turning to powder and that his mother had been contracted to kill him by the Nazis. The voices in his head told him to seek treatment by drinking blood.

Chase's killing spree began on December 29, 1977, when he murdered his first victim, Ambrose Griffin, in a drive-by shooting.

On January 23, 1978, he attacked Theresa Wallin at her home. After shooting the pregnant woman three times, he disemboweled her corpse and drank her blood. Her body was found by her husband that evening.

On January 27, Chase killed his other four victims. Evelyn Miroth and her six-year-old son Jason and her friend Daniel Meredith were babysitting her baby nephew, David Ferreira. When Daniel opened the door to Chase he shot him dead, then he shot Evelyn in the bath, and shot Jason in the head twice before mutilating his dead body. After killing baby David, he fled the scene with the corpse. After canabalizing parts of the body, he dumped it in a nearby graveyard, where it was discovered three months later.

Following a tip-off from one of Chase's neighbors, when the police searched his apartment they found several body parts and brain matter in his fridge; they also found a calendar detailing planned future murder dates—there were forty-four more days still to come.

## BODY COUNT
He killed six people during his one-month killing spree.

## FAMOUS QUOTES
"If the door was locked, that means you're not welcome." (Answer when asked how he selected which houses to break into)

# ADOLFO DE JESUS CONSTANZO

- **BIRTH NAME:** Adolfo de Jesus Constanzo
- **TITLES:** "The Godfather of Matamoros"
- **BIRTH:** November 1, 1962, Miami, Florida, USA
- **DEATH:** May 6, 1989, suicide (he commanded one of his followers to shoot him)

## WHO WAS HE?

He was a serial killer and cult leader in Mexico. The cult sold drugs, held occult ceremonies, and murdered people for use in human sacrifices.

## EARLY INFLUENCES

He was the son of a widowed teenage Cuban immigrant, Delia Aurora Gonzalez del Valle. He was baptized Roman Catholic, but his other major spiritual influences as a child and teenager were Santeria and Palo mayombe— African Diasporic religions, both of which involve animal sacrifice. He made trips to Haiti to be instructed in voodoo and became obsessed with the occult.

## WHAT DID HE DO THAT WAS SO WRONG?

In 1984 he moved to Mexico City and lived in a sex-triangle with a homosexual psychic Jorge Montes and occult-obsessed Omar Orea. Here he gained the status of a high-priest, offering tarot readings, telling the future, and performing ritual cleansing ceremonies involving animal sacrifices, for which he often received thousands of dollars. He became involved with powerful drug dealers and offered them his ritual magic, which by now included the use of human bones robbed from graveyards. Before long he graduated to human sacrifice. He earned tens of thousands of dollars from the drug-dealing Calzada family alone, which funded a lavish lifestyle including a luxury apartment and a fleet of luxury cars. He achieved the status of a god, and his cult even included a doctor and four police officers. Whenever a major drug deal was about to take place, Constanzo would deliver a human sacrifice, and various body parts would be ripped out, boiled and eaten to provide talismanic protection to his drug-dealing clients.

In 1987 he took revenge on the Calzadas when they refused his request for a full partnership in the syndicate. He ritually murdered and mutilated seven members of the household and then turned his affiliation to another drug cartel, the Hernandez family, and the cult's rituals became even more sadistic. However, since most of his victims were part of the world of drug smuggling, it wasn't until the disappearance of a Mark Kilroy, a twenty-one-year-old student at the University of Texas on vacation in Mexico, that Constanzo's killing spree ended. Investigations led the police to his remote ranch where they found an altar and human remains, and a cauldron filled with blood. Police detained several of his followers, who later led them to the graves of fifteen men and boys. Many of the bodies had been decapitated and all of them had been mutilated. Constanzo remained on the run until police cornered him and four of his followers in an apartment in Mexico City on May 6, 1989, and he committed suicide by ordering one of his disciples to shoot him while he embraced his homosexual lover.

## BODY COUNT

No definitive body count has been established, but twenty-three ritual murders have been attributed to him, along with a host of un-solved mutilation murders around Mexico City.

## FAMOUS QUOTES

"They cannot kill you but I can."

"They'll never take me alive."

# MARY ANN COTTON

- **BIRTH NAME:** Mary Ann Cotton
- **TITLES:** "Serial Killer"
- **BIRTH:** October 1832, Low Moorsley, UK
- **DEATH:** March 24, 1873, hanged (executed)

## WHO WAS SHE?

She was an English serial killer, suspected of poisoning up to twenty-one people with arsenic including nine of her own children. Before Harold Shipman, she was the most prolific serial killer in British history.

## EARLY INFLUENCES

She grew up in a strict religious household. Her father, a coal miner, was a strict Methodist and disciplinarian. He fell down a mineshaft and died when Mary Ann was nine. Without an income, the family would have ended up in the dreaded workhouse, if Mary Ann's mother hadn't remarried soon after. Mary Ann had a bad relationship with her stepfather. She left home at sixteen to work as a domestic servant in South Hetton. She was a good worker, but rumors of her promiscuity were rife. Three years later she became a dressmaker and married her first of three husbands, William Mowbray, and had five children within the first four years of their marriage.

## WHAT DID SHE DO THAT WAS SO WRONG?

Childbirth seems to have been the trigger for Mary Ann's killing, perhaps because she was terrified of poverty and the workhouse. Four of her children died in infancy from a mysterious "gastric illness" which afflicted all of her victims. The marriage was unhappy, and the couple argued incessantly about money. William got a job on a steamer, which took him away from home, but he returned in 1865 with an injured foot. Mary Ann nursed him to death and he succumbed to a sudden intestinal disorder. When the doctor visited her home he was surprised to see her already wearing a new dress paid for by her dead husband's life insurance.

Soon after William's death Mary Ann moved her family to Seaham Harbor, where she buried another one of her children. She returned to Sunderland, and became a nurse at the Sunderland Infirmary. She sent her remaining child, Isabella, to live with her grandmother.

There she met and married a patient, George Ward, in August 1865, but he died the following year with chronic stomach trouble.

Mary Ann became housekeeper for a recently widowed shipwright called James Robinson. By Christmas she had poisoned his baby and was soon pregnant by him and they planned to marry. In March of 1867, Mary Ann rushed to the bedside of her sick mother. When she got there she found her mother in much better health, but after a few weeks of Mary Ann's special medicine, she was dead. She picked up Isabella from her grandmother and returned to the Robinson household with her. Within a few weeks Isabella and two more of Robinson's children died of stomach problems. Unsuspecting, Robinson married the pregnant Mary Ann in August (making her a bigamist), and their baby was born in November. Three months later it was dead and James became suspicious, not only of the deaths, but because he discovered that she was running up secret debts, and pestered him to take out life insurance. When he discovered that she had also pawned family valuables he kicked her out of the house.

By 1870 Mary Ann became involved with the brother of a friend, Frederick, a widower with two children. Mary Ann poisoned her friend and became pregnant by Frederick. They married in September, and Mary Ann promptly insured the lives of her new family. She gave birth to her son, Robert in early 1871, and then had an affair with and old flame, Joseph Nattrass, which prompted her to poison Frederick, who died of gastric fever in December. Soon afterwards Mary Ann became pregnant by another man, John Quick Manning. She then poisoned Nattrass along with Frederick's two sons, so that she could clear the decks to marry him.

In July of 1872 Mary Ann poisoned one of Robinson's two sons so that she could collect his life insurance. However Thomas Riley, a local government official, suspected foul play and after a formal inquest discovered arsenic in the dead boy's stomach, a further six other corpses were exhumed and tested positive for poison.

On March 24, 1873, Mary Ann was hanged. The execution was bungled and it took her over three minutes to die.

## BODY COUNT
Mary Ann murdered twenty-one people, including nine of her own children, six stepchildren, three husbands, one lover, and her close friend.

## FAMOUS QUOTES

Mary Ann Cotton
She's dead and she's rotten!
She lies in her bed
With her eyes wide open.

Sing, sing!
Oh, what can I sing?
Mary Ann Cotton is tied up with string.

Where, where?
Up in the air, selling black puddings a penny a pair.

(children's nursery rhyme)

# JEFFREY DAHMER

- **BIRTH NAME:** Jeffrey Dahmer
- **TITLES:** "Serial Killer, Necrophiliac & Cannibal"
- **BIRTH:** May 21, 1960, Milwaukee, Wisconsin, USA
- **DEATH:** November 28, 1994, battered to death by fellow inmate

## WHO WAS HE?

He was an American serial killer, necrophiliac, and cannibal who lured gay and bisexual men back to his house before drugging and killing them.

## EARLY INFLUENCES

His childhood was loving and seemingly normal, except for a double-hernia operation when he was four years old. This traumatized him deeply, because it wasn't explained to him why strangers in white coats were touching his naked body, leaving him feeling exposed and abused. He may also have been abused by an older boy when he was eight.

He reportedly dissected dead animals as a child as well as being painfully introverted. His parents marriage deteriorated over several years until they divorced when he was eighteen, the same year that he committed his first murder.

## WHAT DID HE DO THAT WAS SO WRONG?

His first victim was a nineteen-year-old hitchhiker called Stephen Hicks, whom Dahmer picked up and brought back to his house. After a few drinks, Dahmer hit him with a barbell and strangled him, because he didn't want him to leave. He dismembered and buried the body.

He then spent one term at a university before dropping out. He joined the army but was released after two years because of his excessive drinking and he went to live with his grandmother for six years. In the eighties he was arrested twice for indecent exposure, and served ten months in prison after the second conviction. In 1988 he was convicted of sexually molesting a thirteen-year-old boy, and spent a year in a work release camp with five years probation. During the next two years he killed and dismembered sixteen men whom he had lured back to his house. He tried to turn some of them into sexually compliant "zombies" by drilling holes in their skulls and pouring caustic liquid into the wounds. He had sex with many of the corpses.

One of his victims, a fourteen-year-old, escaped and ran into the road naked, where he was stopped by police officers, who returned him to Dahmer's clutches after he convinced them that they were having a lovers' fight. Later that night Dahmer killed and dismembered him. Had the police bothered to carry out a basic identity check they would have discovered that Dahmer was a convicted sex offender on probation. By the summer of 1991 he was killing approximately one person each week, drugging their drinks before strangling or stabbing them.

On July 22, 1991, he was arrested after one of his victims escaped and led police back to his house, where they found vats of acid which Dahmer used to strip flesh off the bones, photographs of his victims, a freshly severed head in the refrigerator and three in the freezer, and an altar in his bedroom decorated with candles and human skulls. They found several pairs of hands and a penis in a stockpot at the back of a closet. He admitted that he had eaten the bicep of his eighth victim, and said that it tasted like beef.

## BODY COUNT

Dahmer murdered seventeen men and boys between 1978 and 1991. He was sentenced to 943 years in prison.

## FAMOUS QUOTES

"I really screwed up this time."

# FRANÇOIS DUVALIER

- **BIRTH NAME:** François Duvalier
- **TITLES:** "Papa Doc, President for Life"
- **BIRTH:** April 14, 1907, Port-au-Prince, Haiti
- **DEATH:** April 21, 1971, heart attack

## WHO WAS HE?

He was President of Haiti from 1957 and later dictator (President for Life) from 1964 until his death.

## EARLY INFLUENCES

He was born to a family from Martinique and trained as a doctor. In his medical career he was much admired for his work combating yaws, malaria, and typhus amongst the rural population and gained a reputation as a humanitarian. Around the same time he became involved with Le Groupe des Griots, a writers group that believed in Black Nationalism and voodoo. He became leader of the National Health Service in 1946 and Minister of Health three years later. After President Estimé was overthrown in a military coup in 1950, Duvalier became the main opposition leader, and went into hiding until his return in 1957 to win the Haitian election.

## WHAT DID HE DO THAT WAS SO WRONG?

He won the 1957 election with the support of the national army, assassinating key opponents, and using armed gangs. After defeating a coup in 1958 he assembled a group of ruthless thugs to form the "Tonton Macoutes" (Bogeymen). Modeled on the Blackshirts of Fascist Italy, this personal militia purged the army and terrorized the population. His henchmen then consolidated his power with a mixture of violence and voodoo. He created a personality cult, declaring himself to be a voodoo priest and modeled himself upon Baron Samedi, the spirit of the dead.

With corruption endemic the per capita income of the population shrank to $80 and only 10 percent of the country was literate.

In 1964 he declared himself President for Life after a rigged election in which the result was 1.32 million votes for him and not a single vote against. He became a pariah amongst other nations, and was excommunicated in 1966 for harassing the clergy.

When he died in 1971, power passed to his nineteen-year-old son Jean-Claude "Baby Doc" Duvalier, who was as ruthless and corrupt as his father—over half of the government's revenues were embezzled during his time in power.

## BODY COUNT

Estimates for the number of opponents to his regime killed are as high as 30,000.

## FAMOUS QUOTES

"I know the Haitian people because I am the Haitian people."

"I am the personification of the Fatherland. Those who wish to destroy Duvalier wish to destroy the Haitian Fatherland . . . Those who are uncertain about what to do had better keep themselves at my side because a steam roller will crush the opposition and this will be one of the most terrible things that has ever been seen in Haiti."

# ADOLPH EICHMANN

- **BIRTH NAME:** Otto Adolf Eichmann
- **TITLES:** "Little Jew"
- **BIRTH:** March 19, 1906, Solingen, Germany
- **DEATH:** May 31, 1962, hanged (executed)

## WHO WAS HE?

He was a high-ranking Nazi officer who managed the logistics of mass deportation to ghettos and extermination camps in Nazi-occupied Eastern Europe during the Second World War. After the war he eventually fled to Argentina, where he was tracked down and captured by Israeli Mossad agents. He was convicted of crimes against humanity and hanged.

## EARLY INFLUENCES

He was born into a middle-class Protestant family, the son of an industrialist, Karl Adolf Eichmann, who owned a small mining company. As a child Adolf was teased for his dark hair and was nicknamed the "Little Jew." The family moved to Austria after the death of his mother. Adolf studied engineering with a view to entering the family business, but failed. He worked as a laborer and a traveling salesman before joining the Austrian Nazi Party in 1932, and Heinrich Himmler's SS, at that time Hitler's bodyguards.

## WHAT DID HE DO THAT WAS SO WRONG?

In 1933 he became an administrator for the Dachau concentration camp and continued to rise through the ranks of the SS. He was a fanatical anti-Semite and a central figure in the annihilation of the Jews, although at his trial he claimed that he was simply obeying orders. During the 1930s he climbed the Nazi hierarchy, and was instrumental in the deportation, ghettoization, and imprisonment of Jews. In 1939 he was assigned to head RSHA Referat IV D4, the RSHA department that dealt with Jewish affairs and evacuation. His team formulated a plan for mass deportation of Jews, but this was abandoned in favor of the "Final Solution," for which Eichmann became "Transportation Administrator," in charge of all the trains that transported Jews to the death camps. The use of Zyklon-B gas was introduced after Eichmann became concerned that his troops might be affected by having to shoot thousands of people, as well as being a waste of bullets.

## BODY COUNT

He was personally responsible for transporting over two million Jews to their deaths in Auschwitz-Birkenau and other death camps.

## FAMOUS QUOTES

"From my childhood, obedience was something I could not get out of my system. When I entered the armed service . . . it was unthinkable that I would not follow orders."

"To sum it all up, I must say that I regret nothing."

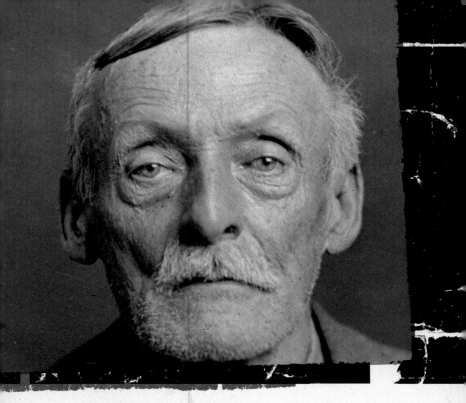

# ALBERT FISH

- **BIRTH NAME:** Hamilton Fish
- **TITLES:** "Gray Man," "Werewolf of Wysteria," "Brooklyn Vampire"
- **BIRTH:** May 19, 1870, Washington, D.C., USA
- **DEATH:** January 16, 1936, electric chair (executed)

## WHO WAS HE?

He was an American serial killer and cannibal who murdered more than fifteen children and tortured up to a hundred others.

## EARLY INFLUENCES

Albert's father died when he was five and he spent most of his life in orphanages, where he was brutally treated, with repeated whippings and where he claimed he "saw boys doing many things they should not have done." As an adult he made a living as a painter and decorator.

Until his mid-forties he appears to have led a relatively normal life, devoted to his wife and six children. However, he had been jailed for grand larceny in 1903 and was arrested subsequently for six petty crimes. After his wife left him when their youngest child was three, he began carrying out some of the most disturbing crimes ever recorded.

## WHAT DID HE DO THAT WAS SO WRONG?

Fish believed that God had chosen him to torture and castrate little boys. Fish bribed children with money or candy, and then when he got them alone he subjected them to rape and brutal torture.

In 1928 he responded to a newspaper advertisement placed by teenager Edward Budd seeking work. Fish, posing as a successful (though shabbily dressed) farmer, gained the confidence of the Budd family before abducting Budd's ten-year-old sister, Grace. He strangled her, then cut her into pieces and cooked and ate her remains over a nine-day period. In a letter which he sent to her mother he claimed, "Sweet and tender she was roasted in the oven."

A year earlier Fish had abducted a four-year-old named Billy Gaffney, whom he tortured: "I cut off his ears, nose, slit his mouth from ear to ear." Then he cooked and ate the rest.

Dr. Fredric Wertham, the psychiatrist who examined him during his trial described Fish as "meek, gentle, benevolent and polite . . . if you wanted someone to entrust your children to, he would be the one you would choose."

## BODY COUNT
He is thought to have raped and tortured over 100 children, and murdered at least fifteen of them.

## FAMOUS QUOTES
"We had lunch. Grace [Budd] sat in my lap and kissed me. I made up my mind to eat her."

"I always had a desire to inflict pain on others and to have others inflict pain on me. I always seemed to enjoy everything that hurt."

"What I did must have been right or an angel would have stopped me, just as an angel stopped Abraham in the Bible."

# FRANCISCO FRANCO

- **BIRTH NAME:** Francisco Paulino Hermenegildo Teódulo Franco y Bahamonde Salgado Pardo
- **TITLES:** "Generalísimo"
- **BIRTH:** December 4, 1892, El Ferrol, Spain
- **DEATH:** November 20, 1975, old age

## WHO WAS HE?

He was the dictator of Spain from 1936 until his death thirty-nine years later.

## EARLY INFLUENCES

Born into an upper-middle-class family, he was the son of a navy paymaster and his mother was a well-known socialite. He joined the army and graduated from military academy in 1910 and quickly gained a reputation as a good officer. By his early twenties he was promoted to become the youngest field grade officer in the Spanish Army. In 1923 King Alfonso XIII was best man at his wedding and three years later he had become the youngest general in Spain.

## WHAT DID HE DO THAT WAS SO WRONG?

He was an ardent royalist, so after the king was deposed he was demoted to military governor of the Canary Islands in February 1936 after the left-wing Popular Front seized power. After being in effective exile for four months, he backed a Nationalist revolution led by Emilio Mola that caused the Spanish Civil War in which half a million people were killed and as many again died from starvation and disease. One of the most notorious incidents in the war was the German carpet bombing of the Basque town of Guernica on April 26, killing 1,654 of its inhabitants and wounding 889.

Franco became the head of the Nationalist Falange Party and with the support of Nazi Germany and Fascist Italy, he became dictator of Spain in March 1939. He banned all other political parties and brutally suppressed all opposition. Hundreds of thousands of Republicans were imprisoned and nearly 200,000 were executed during the next five years. After the war a further half a million Republican refugees fled the country.

Franco introduced the "Nuevo Estado" (New State), system which demanded unquestioning loyalty to the state and denied individual rights and freedoms. He reinstated Catholicism as the state religion, and then his murderous regime was supported and legitimized by the Catholic Church.

## BODY COUNT

A million people died during the Spanish Civil War, and more than 200,000 Republicans were executed afterwards.

## FAMOUS QUOTES

"The war is over, but the enemy is not dead."

"I am responsible only to God and history."

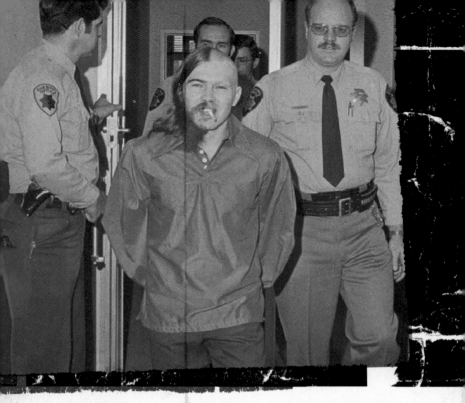

# JOHN LINLEY FRAZIER

- **BIRTH NAME:** John Linley Frazier
- **TITLES:** "Hippie Spree Killer"
- **BIRTH:** 1946, Santa Cruz, California
- **DEATH:** still alive

## WHO WAS HE?

He was a hippie murderer who killed a rich eye surgeon and his family in their home near Santa Cruz in 1970 because he considered them too materialistic.

## EARLY INFLUENCES

Frazier's parents separated when he was two years old and his mother placed him in foster care when he was five. After much delinquent behavior and several spells of juvenile detention, he became a mechanic, got married, and had a child. In 1970 he began taking drugs and received a head trauma in a car accident. Soon afterwards his marriage broke up and Frazier quit his job to become a hippie and became fanatical about ecology and the Tarot.

He was not popular with his hippie associates, because he became increasingly paranoid and full of anger. Eventually he drifted off to live alone in a shack belonging to his mother in the woods in the Soquel hills.

## WHAT DID HE DO THAT WAS SO WRONG?

On October 19, 1970, Frazier broke into the house of wealthy eye surgeon, Victor Ohta, which was a short distance from his shack. The only person at home was his wife, Virginia. Frazier tied her up. When Victor's secretary Dorothy Cadwallader arrived with one of his sons, they were also tied up followed by Victor and his other son when they got home.

Frazier took them outside to the swimming pool and after lecturing them on the ecology and the evils of materialism, he pushed Victor into the pool and shot him three times with a .38 revolver. Then he shot the rest of his captives in the head from behind and threw them in the pool. Forensic tests showed that some of the victims were still alive when they hit the water.

Before leaving, Frazier typed a note on Victor's typewriter and placed it under the windshield wipers of his Rolls-Royce (see below). Then he set fire to the property, and it was this blaze which led the police to the murder scene.

The Ohtas also had two daughters; Taura, eighteen, had left earlier that day to return to college in New York, while her fifteen-year-old sister was at boarding school.

## BODY COUNT

Frazier killed five people.

## FAMOUS QUOTES

"Halloween . . . 1970"

"Today world war 3 will begin as brought to you by the people of the free universe. From this day forward any one and/or company of persons who misuses the natural environment or destroys same will suffer the penalty of death by the people of the free universe."

"I and my comrades from this day forth will fight until death or freedom, against anything or anyone who does not support natural life on this planet, materialism must die or man-kind will."

"KNIGHT OF WANDS
KNIGHT OF CUPS
KNIGHT OF PENTICLES
KNIGHT OF SWORDS"

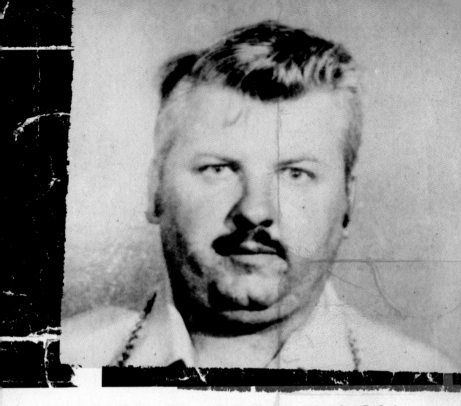

# JOHN WAYNE GACY

- **BIRTH NAME:** John Wayne Gacy, Jr.
- **TITLES:** "Killer Clown"
- **BIRTH:** March 17, 1942, Chicago, Illinois, USA
- **DEATH:** May 10, 1994, lethal injection (executed)

## WHO WAS HE?

He was an American serial killer who was a successful businessman and pillar of his community, and who used to entertain local children's parties in a clown suit.

## EARLY INFLUENCES

He was born and raised in a middle-class Catholic family in Chicago. His father was a violent alcoholic, whom Gacy nevertheless hero-worshipped and from whom he constantly sought approval. At age eleven he suffered a head trauma in a playground accident which caused him to have intermittent blackouts until he was sixteen.

After attending business school he became a shoe salesman in Springfield, Illinois. He married in 1964 and ran a Kentucky Fried Chicken restaurant. Four years later his marriage fell apart after he was convicted of sodomizing a teenage employee. His adored father died while he was in prison, but he was released after serving only eighteen months of a ten-year sentence, and moved back to Illinois, where he hid his criminal record successfully until his arrest thirteen years later for the multiple murders.

He married again (his wife left him in 1976) and built up a successful construction business. He became a prominent and popular member of his church and community, and even became a committee member for the Democratic Party. He also entertained local children in hospitals and parties by dressing up as "Pogo the Clown."

## WHAT DID HE DO THAT WAS SO WRONG?

Between 1972 and 1978 he kidnapped, drugged, raped, tortured, and murdered thirty-three boys and young men. They were young prostitutes, teenage runaways, or young men whom he recruited for his construction business. He buried twenty-nine of them in the crawl space underneath his house, and when he ran out of room he threw five of the bodies into the river. Many of those who attended the huge parties he threw at his house complained of the stench, which Gacy explained away as a mold and moisture problem.

He was caught during a search of his house following the disappearance of a teenage boy in 1978. Police found several items that linked Gacy to earlier crimes, and this led him to confess, although he showed no remorse.

## BODY COUNT

He raped and murdered thirty-three boys and young men aged between nine years old and twenty.

## FAMOUS QUOTES

"You know, clowns can get away with murder."

"You can kiss my ass." (his last words)

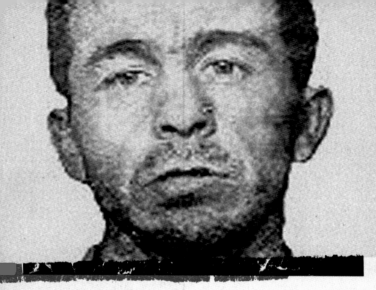

# DONALD GASKINS

- **BIRTH NAME:** Donald Henry Gaskins
- **TITLES:** "Junior Parrott," "Pee Wee"
- **BIRTH:** March 13, 1933, Florence County, South Carolina, USA
- **DEATH:** September 6, 1991, electric chair (executed)

## WHO WAS HE?
He was the most sadistic and prolific serial killer in South Carolina history.

## EARLY INFLUENCES
He was born to a single mother who hooked up with a series of boyfriends and finally a stepfather, all of whom mistreated and beat him. He was nicknamed "Pee Wee" because he was short and skinny. Af-

ter a violent school career, he quit and became a mechanic. As part of a gang called the Trouble Trio he burgled and raped young boys. At age thirteen he attacked a teenage girl with an ax during a burglary and was sent to reform school where he was repeatedly gang raped. He was released in 1951 on his eighteenth birthday but was soon back in prison for attacking a woman with a hammer. He spent the next decade in and out of prison and in the early sixties he was convicted of statutory rape of a twelve-year-old girl. After six more years in prison he was paroled in 1968 and embarked on a career as a serial killer.

## WHAT DID HE DO THAT WAS SO WRONG?

He raped and cannibalized victims, often making them eat parts of their body and keeping them alive for days of torture. After killing his first victim, he described how at this moment he discovered a way to assuage the "bothersome feelings" that had afflicted him his whole life until then.

From then on he threw himself cheerfully into mass murder, performing contract or revenge killings, which he called his "serious murders" and his "coastal killings" which were purely for fun. His victims included his fifteen-year-old niece, and a pregnant mother and her two-year-old toddler.

## BODY COUNT

Although he confessed to thirteen murders, he is thought to have killed as many as two hundred people.

## FAMOUS QUOTES

"I have walked the same path as God, by taking lives and making others afraid, I became God's equal. Through killing others, I became my own master. Through my own power I come to my own redemption . . ."

# LUIS ALFREDO GAVARITO

- **BIRTH NAME:** Luis Alfredo Gavarito
- **TITLES:** "Goofy," "El Loco," "The Priest," The Beast"
- **BIRTH:** January 25, 1957, Génova, Quindío, Colombia
- **DEATH:** still alive

## WHO IS HE?

He is a Colombian serial killer who raped, tortured, and killed 140 children in a five-year killing spree. He is the worst serial killer in the history of South America.

## EARLY INFLUENCES

He was the oldest of seven children, and grew up in the western coffee-growing region of Colombia. As a child he was repeatedly beaten by his father, and he was also raped by two male neighbors. He only received five years of education and left school aged sixteen. He worked as a shop assistant, and then became a street vendor, selling religious icons. He became an alcoholic and received treatment for depression and suicide ideation.

## WHAT DID HE DO THAT WAS SO WRONG?

He committed his first murder in 1992 and then over the next five years he raped, tortured, and killed scores of boys aged between eight and sixteen. Many of his victims were poor or homeless, or the children of street vendors. He gained their trust by giving them gifts and money and took them for a walk. When they got tired he would rape them before cutting their throats. Most of his killings occurred when he was drunk.

He gained access to schools by posing as a representation of fictitious foundations for children or for the aged. He often changed his appearance and lived under an assumed name as he moved around the country: bodies of his victims were discovered in more than sixty towns in a third of Colombia's provinces. He also spent time in Ecuador, and authorities there are still trying to link him with several child murders.

A nationwide manhunt was launched after the bodies of thirty-six of his victims were discovered near the city of Pereira in 1997. At the time police suspected that black magic was involved, or organ trafficking. After an eighteen-month investigation, Gavarito was arrested on December 31, 1998 in the city of Villavicencio for attempting to rape a twelve-year-old boy.

On May 28, 2000, Gavarito unsuccessfully attempted suicide in prison by swallowing a cyanide capsule. Colombia does not have a death penalty, and his crimes were unprecedented. The maximum sentence he could receive was thirty years, and because he had cooperated with police, this has been reduced to twenty-two years. His prison term has become a troubling political issue in Colombia as authorities try to extend his sentence. In late 2006 a judicial review ruled that his sentence could be extended and his release delayed, due to the existence of crimes to which he has not yet confessed.

## BODY COUNT

He confessed to the rape, torture, and murder of 140 victims, but based on skeletons found based on maps Garavito drew in prison, this figure could be as high as 300.

# EDWARD GEIN

- **BIRTH NAME:** Edward Theodore Gein
- **TITLES:** "Butcher of Plainfield," "Plainfield Ghoul"
- **BIRTH:** August 27, 1906, La Crosse, Wisconsin, USA
- **DEATH:** July 26, 1984, respiratory and heart failure

## WHO WAS HE?

He was one of the most notorious grave robbers and murderers in United States history; he made clothing, furniture, and trinkets out of the skin and body parts of his victims, whom he also cannibalized.

## EARLY INFLUENCES

Gein's childhood was abusive and religiously oppressive. His father was a violent alcoholic, and his mother was a religious fanatic who convinced him that sex was dirty and reserved for procreation, and that all women (except her) were whores. She hated her husband so much she made Gein and his brother Henry pray for his death. They grew up on an isolated farm and were not allowed to bring friends home from school, and they became socially awkward.

## WHAT DID HE DO THAT WAS SO WRONG?

In 1943 his brother died in mysterious circumstances during a forest fire (probably hit over the head by Gein). Two years later, devastated by his mother's death, he began robbing graves, targeting middle-aged women who resembled his mother. He took the bodies home and used the skin to create an entire wardrobe.

In November 1957 the police searched Gein's house during an investigation into the death of Bernice Worden. They discovered her body in his shed, hanging upside down and gutted like an animal. In the house they found a mobile made of human lips, a collection of other body parts, a wastebasket and lampshades made of skin, a chair with human arms and upholstered with skin, bedposts made of human skulls, frozen organs in the refrigerator, and soup bowls made out of skulls.

The serial killer Buffalo Bill in Thomas Harris's novel *The Silence of the Lambs* is based on him.

## BODY COUNT

Since most of the body parts found in his house were the result of grave robbing, Gein is believed to have only been responsible for three deaths, those of his brother, Mary Hogan, and Bernice Worden, and to have dug up at least thirteen corpses.

## FAMOUS QUOTES

"Every man's got to have a hobby."

# HERMANN GÖRING

- **BIRTH NAME:** Hermann Wilhelm Göring
- **TITLES:** "Reichsmarschall," "Reichsluftfahrtminister" (Head of the Luftwaffe)
- **BIRTH:** January 12, 1893, Marienbad, Germany
- **DEATH:** October 15, 1946, cyanide poisoning (suicide)

## WHO WAS HE?

He was a leading member of the Nazi Party and commander of the Luftwaffe.

## EARLY INFLUENCES

His father was a professional soldier who rose to become the first governor of German West Africa, which took him away from home during Hermann's early years, which were spent with a governess or with distant relatives. Hermann grew up in two aristocratic castles, belonging to his Jewish godfather Ritter von Eppenstein, which played a major part in developing his romanticized notions of German history. He went to boarding school followed by cadet and military colleges, and joined the Prussian army in 1912, before transferring to the Luftwaffe as a fighter pilot. During the First World War he was shot down and was highly decorated.

## WHAT DID HE DO THAT WAS SO WRONG?

He joined the Nazi Party in 1922 and became an SA commander. He was one of the key members in bringing the Nazis to power and establishing Hitler's dictatorship. He is believed to have masterminded the Reichstag Fire, a pivotal event in the establishment of Nazi Germany. He was appointed head of the Luftwaffe in 1935, and in 1940 Hitler created a special post for him of Reichsmarschall, the highest military rank of the Third Reich.

At the Nuremberg Trials he was tried for war crimes and crimes against humanity and sentenced to death, but he took a cyanide pill a few hours before his execution.

## BODY COUNT

Göring was the highest ranking member of the Nazi Party who had authorized on paper (rather than verbally) the "final solution of the Jewish Question," when he sent a memo to SS Obergruppenführer

Reinhard Heydrich: "submit to me as soon as possible a general plan of the administrative material and financial measures necessary for carrying out the desired final solution of the Jewish question." Between six and twelve million people died in Nazi concentration camps.

## FAMOUS QUOTES

"Naturally the common people don't want war . . . Voice or no voice, the people can always be brought to the bidding of the leaders. That is easy. All you have to do is tell them they are being attacked, and denounce the peacemakers for lack of patriotism and exposing the country to danger. It works the same in any country."

# BELLE GUNNESS

- **BIRTH NAME:** Brynhilde Poulsdatter
- **TITLES:** "Lady Bluebeard"
- **BIRTH:** November 22, 1859, Selbu, Norway
- **DEATH:** c.1931

## WHO WAS SHE?

She was a farmer's widow and serial killer who murdered her suitors for money and buried them in her garden.

## EARLY INFLUENCES

She was born in Norway and emigrated with her husband, Max Sorensen, in her mid-twenties. They ran a homestead in Austin, Illinois, for seventeen years without incident. Belle only turned to crime after the death of her husband in 1900.

## WHAT DID SHE DO THAT WAS SO WRONG?

She sold the farm for $100 and moved to Chicago, where she set up a boarding house. She burned it down before receiving any guests and pocketed the insurance money. She repeated the same crime with a bakery business, before deciding to solve her money worries by re-marrying. She married Peter Gunness and settled with him on his farm in La Porte, Indiana. He died shortly after their wedding in a freak accident: a sausage grinder fell from a high shelf and struck him on the head. This may have been Belle's first murder, since she had a powerful motive: a considerable life insurance payout.

Next she began placing small ads in the newspaper looking for a hus-band. She corresponded with likely applicants, and when she found one who was unattached, with no relatives or friends to miss them, she invited them to her house, on the pretext that he should bring a "deposit" of several thousand dollars to display that his intentions were honest. She killed them and took the money.

She had an accomplice, a farm hand called Roy Lamphere, who helped to dispose of the bodies. On April 28, 1908, Belle's farm was burned to the ground and four charred corpses were discovered, one headless woman, which was identified as Mrs. Gunness, and three children. Police dug up fourteen male corpses, and Lamphere was charged with arson. He later confessed that the headless woman wasn't Belle, but a female vagrant. Belle had faked her death and was never brought to justice.

## BODY COUNT

The bodies of fourteen victims were discovered at her farm, and she was probably responsible for the death of her first and second hus-bands, the three children and female vagrant, although there may have been many more bodies undiscovered around the farm.

## FAMOUS QUOTES

"Rich, good-looking widow, young, owner of a large farm, wishes to get in touch with a gentleman of wealth with cultured tastes. Object, matrimony."

# ABIMAEL GUZMÁN

- **BIRTH NAME:** Manuel Rubén Abimael Guzmán Reynoso
- **TITLES:** "President Gonzalo," "Shampoo"
- **BIRTH:** December 3, 1934, Mollendo, Peru
- **DEATH:** still alive

## WHO IS HE?

He is the former leader of the brutal Maoist guerrilla group in Peru commonly known as Sendero Luminoso, "Shining Path," which is on the U.S. Department of State's list of "Designated Foreign Terrorist Organizations."

On September 12, 1992, he was captured during a raid of a safe house in Lima. He is currently serving life imprisonment at San Lorenzo Island naval base, near Lima.

## EARLY INFLUENCES

He was born in Mollendo, about 600 miles south of Lima, the illegitimate son of a wealthy merchant. His mother died when he was five years old and he was brought up first by his mother's family and later at a private Catholic secondary school. In his late teens he studied philosophy and law at San Agustin National University in Arequipa, where he was described by his peers as shy, disciplined, and obsessive. In his late twenties he became a professor of philosophy at San Cristobal of Huamanga University in the central Peruvian Andes, where he became increasingly politicized and committed to bringing about revolution in Peru. When the Peruvian Communist Party fragmented during the 1960s, Guzmán became leader of one faction, the "Shining Path," with the aim of a peasant-led revolution on the Maoist model.

# WHAT DID HE DO THAT WAS SO WRONG?

For nearly thirty years, Guzmán was the party strategist of the Shining Path and he developed a personality cult around himself. By 1980 the Shining Path has developed into a Maoist terrorist guerrilla movement and it launched its armed fight on May 17 by raiding polling stations and burning ballot boxes in the rural town of Chuschi, high in the Peruvian Andes, to disrupt democratic elections.

Its influence grew until it controlled large areas of central and southern Peru and conducted numerous attacks around Lima. For a decade it was the cause of much violence and bloodshed, with indiscriminate bombings, assassinations, kidnappings, and bank robberies. Its victims and opponents were often hacked to death with machetes.

## BODY COUNT

The civil war that resulted from the activities of the Shining Path led to the deaths of over 70,000 people.

## FAMOUS QUOTES

"Long live the Communist Party of Peru! Glory to Marxism-Leninism-Maoism! Glory to the Peruvian people! Long live the heroes of the people's war!"

"We see worldwide Maoism is marching relentlessly forward in its task of leading the new wave of the world proletarian revolution."

# ROBERT HANSEN

- **BIRTH NAME:** Robert Tårnesvik Hansen
- **TITLES:** "Swede"
- **BIRTH:** February 15, 1939, Estherville, Iowa, USA
- **DEATH:** still alive

## WHO IS HE?

He is an American serial killer who flew his female victims into the Alaskan wilds and hunted them down like wild game.

## EARLY INFLUENCES

His father was a Danish immigrant baker, and very strict. Robert was made to work long hours in the bakery. In his adolescence he was short, covered in acne, had a pronounced stutter, and was unpopular at school. A left-hander, he was forced to use his right hand, which made his difficulties even more profound. After graduating from high school he enlisted in the Army Reserves, where he received basic training.

When he was twenty-one, shortly after getting married he burned down the school bus garage. He was sentenced to three years in prison and his wife left him. He was released after twenty months with a strong urge to get even. He married again in 1963 and after being arrested several more times for petty theft he moved with his new wife to Anchorage, Alaska, in 1967. Here he became a well-liked member of the community and won several hunting trophies. However, by the late seventies he was imprisoned for stealing a chain saw and was placed on lithium after being diagnosed with bipolar disorder. After his release a year later he set up his own bakery using money from a fake theft insurance claim.

## WHAT DID HE DO THAT WAS SO WRONG?

After spending the seventies hiring prostitutes and then raping them, he started killing them at the beginning of the eighties. In 1982 he bought a small airplane, and although he never gained his license, he used it to fly his victims out to the Knik River, where he shot them with a .223-caliber Mini-14 rifle (he had a collection of over twenty rifles) and/or stabbed them with a hunting knife. On several occasions he released the women into the wilderness and then hunted them down like wild animals.

Back at home he kept animal trophies upstairs and those from his human victims in the basement, including items of jewelry, ID cards, and newspaper clippings. It was these that helped secure a conviction, after one of his victims escaped in June 1983 and went to the police.

He pleaded guilty to four murders, and provided the location of twelve other grave sites in the Knik River Valley from which seven bodies were recovered. He was sentenced to 461 years in prison plus life without chance of parole.

## BODY COUNT

Hansen has been linked with sixteen murders and at least thirty rapes, but it is possible that he killed twice this number.

## FAMOUS QUOTES

"He sort of looked like the perfect dork." (one of his rape victims)

"To big game hunter Robert Hansen, Alaska was paradise. But for his victims, it was a terrifying wilderness where no one could hear their screams." (Bernard DuClos)

# ERIC HARRIS &
# DYLAN KLEBOLD

- **BIRTH NAME:** Eric David Harris
- **TITLES:** "Columbine Killer"
- **BIRTH:** April 9, 1981, Wichita, Kansas, USA
- **DEATH:** April 20, 1999, shot (suicide)

**BIRTH NAME:** Dylan Bennet Klebold

**TITLES:** "Columbine Killer"

**BIRTH:** September 11, 1981, Lakewood, Colorado, USA

**DEATH:** April 20, 1999, shot (suicide)

## WHO WERE THEY?

They were the high school seniors who were perpetrators of the Columbine High School massacre in Jefferson County, Colorado, on April 20, 1999.

## EARLY INFLUENCES

Harris was the son of a retired US Air Force pilot. His brother Kevin was an A student and played for the football team, sparking theories that sibling rivalry played a part in his troubled psyche. They moved five times during his childhood, making Eric the new kid in school and in his own words "the bottom of the food chain."

Klebold's father was a realtor, and his mother was an employment counselor. They lived in Deer Creek Canyon, south of Lakewood. Both boys had been the target of bullying, but they idea that they were complete outsiders appears to be a myth that has circulated since the shootings. They were members of a group of Goths who called themselves the "Trenchcoat Mafia."

## WHAT DID THEY DO THAT WAS SO WRONG?

Even before they carried out the massacre, there were warning signs that they were dangerous. They had posted messages on Harris's Web site describing pipe bomb tests, and they made a death threat against a fellow student. They had also made a video together for a school project showing them pretending to shoot fake guns in the school corridors, and in 1988 they had been arrested for criminal trespassing and theft, after which Harris attended anger management classes.

Their plan was to kill 250 students and teachers, then walk through the neighborhood shooting more victims before hijacking an airplane and crashing it in the middle of New York City.

At 11:14 A.M. Harris and Klebold walked into the school armed with two sawn-off shotguns, a rifle, a TEC-9 semi-automatic handgun, a 9mm semi-automatic rifle, and several homemade bombs, two of which they placed in the school cafeteria.

Five minutes later, after shouting "Go! Go!" they began firing at fellow students. At 11:25 A.M. the police arrive in time to hear the first of two pipe bomb explosions in the cafeteria. Made from small propane tanks, if they had detonated properly the library upstairs would have collapsed onto the cafeteria, killing and injuring over 600 people. In this respect they failed in their mission to outdo the Waco and Oklahoma City bombings, as described in Harris's journal, which was later discovered by police in his bedroom. After their abortive killing spree Harris and Klebold committed suicide in the school library.

## BODY COUNT
They killed twelve classmates and one teacher and wounded twenty-four others.

## FAMOUS QUOTES
"We're hoping. We're hoping. I hope we kill 250 of you. It will be the most nerve-racking 15 minutes of my life, after the bombs are set and we're waiting to charge through the school. Seconds will be like hours. I can't wait. I'll be shaking like a leaf." (Klebold)

"We're going to die doing it." (Harris)

# HEINRICH HIMMLER

- **BIRTH NAME:** Heinrich Luitpold Himmler
- **TITLES:** "Reichsführer-SS," "Chief of the German Police in the Ministry of the Interior"
- **BIRTH:** October 7, 1900, Munich, Germany
- **DEATH:** May 23, 1945, cyanide poisoning (suicide)

## WHO WAS HE?

He was the Commander of the German Schutzstaffel (SS) and the second most powerful man in Nazi Germany.

## EARLY INFLUENCES

He was born to a Bavarian middle-class family and had a normal upbringing; his father was secondary school teacher. When the First World War began Heinrich begged his parents to allow him to become an officer, but they refused. After leaving school in 1918 he trained with the eleventh Bavarian Regiment but he was not very athletic, and was discharged. During his late teens he developed a belief in the racial superiority of the Aryan race, and felt that God had chosen the Germans to rule the world.

## WHAT DID HE DO THAT WAS SO WRONG?

He joined the SS in 1925, and four years later became its commander (Reichsführer-SS). He built the organization from 280 members to over 52,000 by the time the Nazis came to power in 1933. He was instrumental in the "Night of the Long Knives" in June 1934 when SA commander Ernst Röhm and many of Hitler's opponents and personal enemies were murdered. Himmler later became the Chief of German Police and Minister of the Interior and organized the secret police (Gestapo).

He was responsible for organizing Germany's regime of concentration camps and became one of the main architects of the Holocaust.

He committed suicide by biting a cyanide capsule after he was captured by the Allies.

## BODY COUNT

Himmler oversaw the industrial-scale extermination of between six and twelve million people.

## FAMOUS QUOTES

"I am talking about the evacuation of the Jews, the extermination of the Jewish people. It is one of those things that one talks of easily." (Posen speech, October 4, 1943)

# ADOLF HITLER

- **BIRTH NAME:** Adolf Hitler
- **TITLES:** "The Führer"
- **BIRTH:** April 20, 1889, Braunau, Austria
- **DEATH:** April 30, 1945, cyanide tablet (suicide)

## WHO WAS HE?

He was the leader of the National Socialist German Workers Party (Nationalsozialistische Deutsche Arbeiterpartei or Nazi Party).

## EARLY INFLUENCES

Hitler's parents came from poor peasant families. His father was very strict and beat him when he was disobedient. He did extremely well at primary school but became a slacker at secondary level and left without graduating. Deeply religious, he briefly considered becoming a monk. By age eighteen he had resolved to become an artist, but rejection by the Vienna Academy of Art left him devastated. However, he stayed in Vienna and pretended to his mother that he was an art student, while living off his dead father's pension. He evaded military call-up for four years, and in 1914 he failed his medical: "unfit for combatant and auxiliary duty—too weak. Unable to bear arms." He eventually joined up during the First World War and distinguished himself as a dispatch runner, earning five medals, including the prestigious Iron Cross. In 1919 he joined the German Worker's Party (which later became the National Socialist German Workers Party or Nazi Party), where he developed his powers of oratory and became a passionate and influential speaker.

During the early 1930s Hitler exploited high unemployment and fear of Communism to increase public support for his party until he became Chancellor in January 1933, despite having only a third of the seats in the Reichstag. Meanwhile, Göring, his minister for interior, sacked senior officials such as high-ranking police officers and replaced them with Nazi supporters. After a fire at the Reichstag, Hitler was able to assume dictatorial powers, declaring all other political parties illegal, so that by the end of 1933 over 150,000 political prisoners were in newly opened concentration camps. Germany became a fascist state. Hitler systematically purged all opposition, including the paramilitary wing of the Nazi Party, the Sturmabteilung (SA; also known as storm troopers or brownshirts) during the "Night of the Long Knives" on June 30, 1934.

## WHAT DID HE DO THAT WAS SO WRONG?

Hitler believed that Aryan superiority was threatened in particular by the Jewish race, which he felt was responsible for everything that was wrong with Germany. He was convinced that Jews and Communists were trying to take over the world.

On November 9 and 10, 1938, the Nazi-engineered "Kristallnacht" (Crystal Night) took place, ostensibly as a reaction to the murder of a German diplomat by a young Jewish refugee. Over 7,500 Jewish shops were destroyed and 400 synagogues were burned down. Twenty thousand Jews were sent to concentration camps. On September 1, 1939, Germany, led by Adolf Hitler and the Nazi Party, invaded Poland, starting the Second World War.

## BODY COUNT

Over sixty million people were killed during the Second World War and Hitler's racial policies culminated in the genocide of twelve million people, including six million Jews, in the Holocaust.

## FAMOUS QUOTES

"Every manifestation of human culture, every product of art, science and technical skill, which we see before our eyes today, is almost exclusively the product of Aryan creative power."

"A highly intelligent man should take a primitive and stupid woman."

"By means of shrewd lies, unremittingly repeated, it is possible to make people believe that heaven is hell—and hell heaven. The greater the lie, the more readily it will be believed."

# ENVER HOXHA

- **BIRTH NAME:** Enver Hoxha
- **TITLES:** "Supreme Comrade-Chairman-Prime Minister-Foreign-Minister-Minister of War-Commander-in-Chief of the People's Army Enver Hoxha," "Great Teacher," "Sole Force"
- **BIRTH:** October 16, 1908, Gjirokastër, Albania
- **DEATH:** April 11, 1985, heart attack

## WHO WAS HE?

He was the Marxist-Leninist dictator of Albania from the end of the Second World War until his death in 1985.

## EARLY INFLUENCES

He was born into a wealthy Muslim family; his father was a cloth merchant, and his uncle, Hysen Hoxha, was a major political influence during his childhood: he was an activist involved in the declaration of Albanian independence which took place when Enver was four.

After attending Albania's best schools he won a scholarship to the University of Montpellier in France. He dropped out and moved to Paris, where he studied philosophy at the Sorbonne and became a committed Marxism-Leninist, and a big admirer of Stalin. He returned to Albania and became a teacher, but was sacked in 1939 when the country was occupied by the Italians and he refused to join the Albanian Fascist Party. He founded and became leader of the Albanian Communist party in 1941 and ran a tobacco shop in Tirana while co-coordinating the Albanian resistance movement, which took power in 1944 after the Italians and Germans left, and Hoxha became prime minister.

## WHAT DID HE DO THAT WAS SO WRONG?

As soon as he came to power he conducted trials of those who had collaborated with the Fascists, and managed to eliminate much of his political opposition along the way. Throughout his rule he had repeated purges to eliminate political opponents.

He then confiscated all farmland from wealthy landowners and herded people into large collectives or factories and began a wide-scale industrialization program, intended to make Albania self-sufficient. He closed borders to the outside world, stopped citizens from traveling abroad, and pretended that communism was turning Albania into an advanced industrialized nation. In practice the country became more and more backward, even by Eastern Bloc standards. Living conditions were very low, and people didn't even have access to basic amenities such as telephones.

The country had a population of only three million people, but paranoid Hoxha had 600,000 one-man pillbox bunkers built, at great expense, to protect the country against possible invasion by the United States.

He organized a personality cult around him and in 1967 he declared the country to be the first officially atheist state. He destroyed and confiscated places of worship and all forms of cultural and religious expression became illegal. Anyone found in possession of a holy book such as the Bible or Koran was imprisoned in forced labor camps. His secret police network (called the "Sigurimi" and modeled on the Russian KGB), was so extensive that over one-third of the country's population had spent time either in prison camp or had been brutally interrogated.

## BODY COUNT
He killed thousands of people during repeated purges and imprisoned a significant percentage of the Albanian population.

## FAMOUS QUOTES
"I knew and shall always remember my father as model parent and far-sighted leader, determined to defend victories achieved. He was a genuine democrat—never a dictator." (Ilir Hoxha, his son)

# SADDAM HUSSEIN

- **BIRTH NAME:** Saddam Hussein Abd al-Majid al-Tikriti
- **TITLES:** "President of Iraq"
- **BIRTH:** April 28, 1937, Al-Awja, Iraq
- **DEATH:** December 30, 2006 (hanged)

## WHO WAS HE?

He was President of Iraq from 1979 until April 9, 2003.

## EARLY INFLUENCES

He was a rural peasant boy, born into a family of shepherds. He never knew his father, who left his mother six months before he was born. He spent the first three years of his life with the family of his maternal uncle, because his mother was suffering from severe depression. His mother remarried, and when Saddam returned home he was treated brutally by his stepfather. At age ten he went to live with another uncle, who was a militant Iraqi nationalist. Saddam would later married her daughter, and kill her brother by sabotaging his helicopter.

When he was twenty he joined the revolutionary Ba'ath Party. The following year Iraq's King Faisal II was overthrown in a coup led by General Abdul Karim Qassim. Saddam and the Ba'ath party opposed the new government, and with US assistance they tried to assassinate Qassim. During the operation Saddam was shot in the leg, and the CIA pulled him out of the country and gave him training in Beirut and supported him during his exile. With US arms and intelligence the Ba'ath party finally overthrew Qassin in 1963 and Saddam returned from exile and became a leading party member, and after another coup, became deputy to the President.

In those early years Saddam modernized the country and implemented large-scale social services campaigns to educate Iraq's population, and introduced a free public health systems and subsidies for farmers. He received awards from the UN for his progressive initiatives, and gained wide appeal throughout Iraq. In the 1970s the West supported Saddam with weapons and intelligence, since he was considered to be a bulwark against communism and Islamic fundamentalism. Saddam became President in 1979, but had already been Iraq's de facto leader for many years.

## WHAT DID HE DO THAT WAS SO WRONG?

As soon as he came to power he called an assembly of the Ba'ath party and read out a list of sixty-eight party members who he claimed were plotting against him. He had them tried and executed for treason. Then he brutally suppressed all opposition and created a personality cult, with thousands of portraits, posters, and statues of him erected all over Iraq.

His biggest opponents to his policies of pan-Arabism and modernization, were the Kurds of northern Iraq and the separatist movement there. He used chemical weapons to suppress the Kurds, and killed thousands of Shiites in southern Iraq. He tortured and murdered thousands more of his own people. An Amnesty International report details extensive beatings and torture.

With US support he started an eight-year war with Iran, by invading Khuzestan on September 22, 1980. During the war, Iraq used US-supplied chemical weapons on Kurdish separatists, and on March 16, 1988, the Kurdish town of Halabja was attacked with mix of mustard gas and nerve agents, killing 5,000 civilians, and injuring 10,000 more.

Saddam was left with a war debt of roughly $75 billion borrowed from other Arab countries, of which $30 billion was from Kuwait. Kuwait was keeping oil prices low by pumping large amounts of oil, but Saddam needed high oil prices to rebuild his country, so he invaded Kuwait on August 2, 1990, causing the First Gulf War. After a US-led coalition drove him out of Kuwait in February 1991, Saddam ordered his retreating men to set fire to over 600 Kuwaiti oil wells, and destroy infrastructure, leading to the loss of sixty million barrels of oil and wide-scale pollution.

After the war the UN sanctions placed upon Iraq crippled the country. Saddam continued living in luxury, moving between his 100 palaces, while his people starved.

## BODY COUNT

Thousands of Kurds and Sunnis were killed by his regime, and he tortured and murdered thousands more of his own people. The Iran-Iraq war caused upwards of 1.7 million deaths on both sides.

He was executed December 30, 2006.

## FAMOUS QUOTES

"We are ready to sacrifice our souls, our children and our families so as not to give up Iraq. We say this so no one will think that America is capable of breaking the will of the Iraqis with its weapons."

"I do not respond to this so-called court, with all due respect to its people, and I retain my constitutional right as the president of Iraq. Neither do I recognize the body that has designated and authorized you, nor the aggression, because all that has been built on false basis is false."

# JAVED IQBAL

- **BIRTH NAME:** Javed Iqbal
- **TITLES:** "Serial Killer"
- **BIRTH:** unknown
- **DEATH:** October 7, 2001, strangled

## WHO WAS HE?

He was a serial killer operating in Lahore, Pakistan, who drugged, raped and killed 100 boys during an eighteen-month period and dissolved their dead bodies in acid.

## EARLY INFLUENCES

Little is known about Iqbal's childhood, but he is believed to be a twice divorced father of two. He committed his crimes when he was in his mid-forties. He appeared a paternal, harmless looking man with a shock of white hair and glasses.

## WHAT DID HE DO THAT WAS SO WRONG?

He found boys on the street, gained their confidence, brought them back to his flat, then drugged, raped, and strangled them with an iron chain. He disposed of their bodies by dissolving them in vat of hydrochloric acid outside his house. Once the remains were liquefied he poured the sludge into the sewer, until neighbors complained of the smell, when he switched to the Tavi River. He kept trophies such as clothing and shoes.

Once Iqbal reached his kill target he turned himself in to police on December 30, 1999, and claimed he could have killed 500 boys without detection if he wished. Only one-quarter of the street boys had been reported missing. Before going to the police Iqbal had confessed his crimes by sending a letter to the local newspaper, sparking the largest manhunt in Pakistani history, which had still been unable to track him down.

His reason for the killings was that he had been beaten almost to death by two of the boys he had invited into his house. This had left him with head injuries and depression, and it had led to the death of his mother. His killing spree was intended to avenge his mother's death. Another reason was that he claimed he wanted to highlight the plight of street urchins.

He was sentenced to be strangled to death with the same chain he used to kill the children. The judge decreed that his body would then be cut into 100 pieces and dissolved in acid. Before the sentence could be carried out Iqbal was found strangled with his bed sheets in his prison cell. He had been beaten with a blunt instrument, so his death was most likely a murder, rather than suicide. The prison guard claimed to have been asleep when the death occurred.

## BODY COUNT

Iqbal claimed to have killed 100 boys, but only the remains of two of his victims have been found. However, evidence of more was recovered from his house, including eighty-five pairs of shoes.

## FAMOUS QUOTES

"I am Javed Iqbal, killer of 100 children . . . I hate this world, I am not ashamed of my action and I am ready to die. I have no regrets. I killed 100 children."

"It cost me 120 rupees [about $2.40 US] to erase each victim."

# JACK THE RIPPER

- **BIRTH NAME:** Likely candidates include Montague John Druitt, Severin Klosowski, Walter Sickert, Prince Albert Duke of Clarence, Sir William Gull
- **TITLES:** "Jack the Ripper," "The Whitechapel Murderer"
- **BIRTH:** unknown
- **DEATH:** unknown

## WHO WAS HE?

He was an unidentified serial killer who killed and mutilated five prostitutes in the Whitechapel area of London in 1888. Speculation about his true identity continues to this day. He was left-handed and many eyewitnesses testify to seeing a man of medium height with light hair and a full moustache. Some have suggested he had surgical or medical knowledge owing to the incisions.

## WHAT DID HE DO THAT WAS SO WRONG?

He targeted prostitutes during the hours of darkness in public or semi-public places, cutting the victim's throat and then often mutilating the body. He may have strangled them first.

His first victim, forty-two-year-old Mary Ann "Polly" Nichols, had her throat cut across as deep as the spinal chord.

A week later the second victim, Annie Chapman, was found with her entrails scattered around her. The head had been severed so deeply it was attached only by a flap of skin. Two brass rings and two bright new coins had been placed near her feet and a leather apron was found nearby, leading some to suspect Masonic links.

The third victim, Elizabeth Stride, had her throat cut and an attempt had been made to cut off her ear.

The Ripper removed and kept a kidney from the fourth victim, Catherine "Kate" Eddowes.

Finally, six weeks after the killing spree had begun, he claimed his final victim, Mary Jane Kelly, mutilating her more completely than the others. He skinned her face, removed ears and nose and slit her throat from ear to ear. The left arm was attached to the shoulder by skin alone. The internal organs were placed around the body.

## BODY COUNT

Five murders have definitely been attributed to him, but he may have been responsible for the deaths of at least three other prostitutes.

## FAMOUS QUOTES

"Dear Boss, I keep on hearing the police have caught me but they won't fix me just yet . . . I am down on whores and I shan't quit ripping them till I do get buckled." (Excerpt from a letter received by the Central News Agency on 29 September 1888)

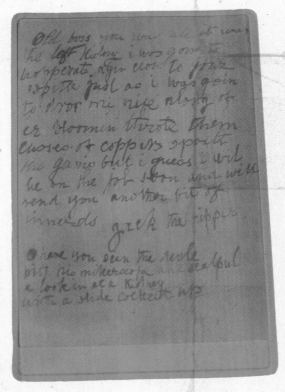

# REVEREND JIM JONES

- **BIRTH NAME:** James Warren Jones
- **TITLES:** "Father"
- **BIRTH:** May 13, 1931, Crete, Indiana, USA
- **DEATH:** November 18, 1978, shot (suicide)

## WHO WAS HE?

He was the founder and leader of the Peoples Temple church that later turned into a doomsday cult, resulting in the mass suicide of its followers.

## EARLY INFLUENCES

Jim Jones was the son a Klan member. From an early age he had a fascination with death, and he enjoyed torturing and killing small animals. As a child he was indoctrinated by a Christian fundamentalist friend. This mix of religion and morbidity later proved a lethal combination.

As a young adult he became a preacher and sold monkeys door to door to raise enough money to found his own church. He called it the Wings of Deliverance, and later the Peoples Temple. He appeared to be a respectable figure: he was ordained by a mainstream Christian organization and his church was based on racial equality, and his equal treatment of African Americans was unheard of at the time. However, things began to go badly wrong for his church after it was investigated for tax evasion and he and his followers moved to South America.

## WHAT DID HE DO THAT WAS SO WRONG?

Jones considered himself the reincarnation of both Jesus and Lenin, made worse by his heavy use of LSD, and barbiturates. He settled in Guyana, South America, with 1,000 of his followers (the majority of whom were black), in 4,000 acres of jungle, which his church had rented and named Jonestown. Shortly afterwards there were reports of mass beatings and even murder, so in November 1978, US Congressman Leo Ryan led a fact-finding mission to Jonestown. They interviewed cult members for three days before deciding to leave on November 18 after an attempt was made on Ryan's life. They took with them about twenty cult members who wanted to escape.

However, a bunch of Jones's armed guards followed them to the airstrip and open fire, killing five of their party. Later that day, all the cult members committed mass "revolutionary" suicide. Most died after drinking Fla-Vor-Aid poisoned with potassium cyanide and tranquilizers, others were shot. The children were killed first, and babies had cyanide squirted into their mouths. Jones either shot himself, or ordered one of his followers to do it.

The suicide had been planned: Jones had already developed an idea called "Translation," in which his followers would move to another planet after death, and they had already rehearsed with pretend suicides rituals.

## BODY COUNT
A total of 914 inhabitants of Jonestown died, 276 of them children, and 5 men were killed at the airstrip.

## FAMOUS QUOTES
"I am the Way, the Truth, and the Light. No one can come to the Father but through me."

"If we can't live in peace then let's die in peace. We are not committing suicide—it's a revolutionary act."

# RADOVAN KARADŽIĆ

- **BIRTH NAME:** Radovan Karadžić
- **TITLES:** "Head of State, Serbian Republic of Bosnia and Herzegovina"
- **BIRTH:** June 19, 1945, Petnjica, Yugoslavia
- **DEATH:** still alive

## WHO IS HE?
He is the former Bosnian Serb leader alleged to have sanctioned concentration camps, torture, rape, and massacres of civilians during the 1992–95 war.

## EARLY INFLUENCES
His father, Vuk, was a former member of a group of Serb nationalist guerrillas who fought against the Nazis and he spent most of Radovan's childhood in jail. In 1960 Radovan moved to Sarajevo to study medicine and became a psychologist in the Koševo Hospital. He was also a poet, and it was the Serb nationalist writer Dobrica Cosic, who encouraged him to go into politics.

In 1989 he helped set up the Serbian Democratic Party in Bosnia-Herzegovina, which aimed to join the Republic's Serb with Croatian Serbs to form a Greater Serbia with Serbia and Montenegro. On April 6, 1992, the Serbian Republic of Bosnia and Herzegovina was recognized by the UN as an independent state and he became its leader.

## WHAT DID HE DO THAT WAS SO WRONG?

He is accused of having ordered the ethnic cleansing of Bosniaks and Croats. Since 1996, after the Dayton accord that ended the Bosnian war, he has been a fugitive, one of the most wanted men in the world for war crimes and genocide by the International Criminal Tribunal for the former Yugoslavia in The Hague. His ability to evade arrest for so long has made him a hero among the Bosnian Serbs.

International pressure to apprehend Karadžić intensified in 2005 after the surrender of several of his former generals, and footage of captives from Srebrenica being executed by Bosnian Serb soldiers was aired on television in the former Yugoslavia.

## BODY COUNT

The UN claims his army killed at least 7,500 Muslim men and boys from Srebrenica in July 1995 as part of an operation intended to "terrorize and demoralize the Bosnian Muslim and Bosnian Croat population." He is also accused of the shelling of Sarajevo, and using 284 UN peacekeepers as human shields in 1995.

About 550,000 ethnic Croats were displaced from their homes during the Yugoslav wars.

## FAMOUS QUOTES

"Everything goes really well, all of my orders are carried out, and even [my] personal relationship with General Mladic has improved, so there is no threat that there will be disarray in the Serbian republic."

"If The Hague was a real juridical body I would be ready to go there to testify or do so on television, but it is a political body that has been created to blame the Serbs."

# EDMUND KEMPER

- **BIRTH NAME:** Edmund Kemper III
- **TITLES:** "The Co-ed Killer"
- **BIRTH:** December 18, 1948, Burbank, California, USA
- **DEATH:** still alive

## WHO IS HE?

He is a serial killer who operated in the Santa Cruz, California, area during the early 1970s, killing and dismembering young female hitchhikers.

## EARLY INFLUENCES

Kemper's parents divorced when he was young and he had a very bad relationship with his mother, whom Kemper felt was excessively controlling. The warning signs of his future crimes were present during childhood: he enjoyed torturing animals and playing "gas chamber" with his sister, who would pull the imaginary execution lever making Kemper thrash around in agonized death throes. He was made to sleep in the basement, a cold and damp place that gave him nightmares, and Kemper believes, contributed to his violent behavior.

## WHAT DID HE DO THAT WAS SO WRONG?

Kemper committed his first murders when he was fifteen, when he shot and stabbed his grandmother, then killed his grandfather when he returned home, so that he wouldn't have to find his wife's dead body. His motive was that he "just wanted to see what it felt like to kill Grandma and Grandpa."

He was sent to Atascadero State Hospital where despite being diagnosed as a sociopath, he managed to convince the authorities that he was a Bible-reading reformed character who wanted to make amends (he had a measured IQ close to that of a genius).

After his release he began picking up female hitchhikers and taking them to their destination, in rehearsal for being a kidnapper. In 1972 he stopped rehearsing and killed six hitchhikers. He had sex with their corpses, cut them up, and kept their heads as souvenirs. He also ate some of their flesh in a macaroni and cheese casserole. He buried the head of one of his victims in his mother's garden because he claimed his mother "always wanted people to look up to her."

In April 1973 he beat his sleeping mother to death with a hammer, decapitated her, and used her head as a dartboard. Then he invited over one of her friends, killed her and had sex with her corpse. Afterwards he turned himself into the police, saying that he should suffer "death by torture."

## BODY COUNT
Kemper killed ten people, including three members of his family.

## FAMOUS QUOTES
"I had thought of annihilating the entire block that I lived on."

# GENGHIS KHAN

- **BIRTH NAME:** Temüjin Borjigin
- **TITLES:** "Khan of Mongol Empire"
- **BIRTH:** c. 1162, Hentiy, Mongolia
- **DEATH:** August 18, 1227, after a fall from his horse

## WHO WAS HE?

He was the thirteenth-century Mongol military leader and founder of the Mongol Empire that made up two-thirds of the known world until his death. He united the Central Asian confederations and gave them a common identity, for which he is remembered as the Father of Mongolia. One in 200 modern Mongolians is related to him (he has more than seventeen million direct descendants).

## EARLY INFLUENCES

Legend says that as a newborn he had a blood clot in the palm of his hand, an omen that he was destined to be a hero. He had a hard childhood. His father was poisoned by the neighboring Tartars when Genghis was nine years old, giving him a claim to be his clan's chief. The clan abandoned him and his family because they didn't want to be ruled by a boy. For the next few years he and his family lived an impoverished nomad life. This hard life taught him vital survival skills. He murdered his half-brother Bekhter in an argument over food and expressed no remorse, despite a good ticking off from his mother.

## WHAT DID HE DO THAT WAS SO WRONG?

He ruled the state he had conquered, notably the Chinese and Persians, with utter ruthlessness. He massacred entire cities that resisted him as a way of frightening others into submission. Those who surrendered were spared violence, but those who resisted were brutally slaughtered. In 1221 his army killed 1,748,000 people at Nishapur in one hour. Khan convinced the city commander that Mongols would stop attacking if the city sent out 1,000 cats and several thousand swallows. When he got them, Genghis had bits of cloth tied to their tails and set the cloth on fire. The cats and birds fled back to the city and ended up setting hundreds of fires inside the city. Then Genghis attacked and won.

Despite his brutality, he did introduce laws to protect women from being kidnapped, to capitally punish the stealing of livestock, and he regulated hunting, improving the availability of meat for everyone.

## BODY COUNT

Estimates range between forty and sixty million people across Asia and Europe; while he undoubtedly exaggerated the figures, tens of millions is not unrealistic.

## FAMOUS QUOTES

"Man's greatest good fortune is to chase and defeat his enemy, seize his total possessions, leave his married women weeping and wailing, ride his gelding, use his women as a nightshirt and support.

# AYATOLLAH KHOMEINI

- **BIRTH NAME:** Ruhollah Mousaui
- **TITLES:** "Grand Ayatollah"
- **BIRTH:** May 17, 1900, Khomeyn, Iran
- **DEATH:** June 3, 1989, cancer

## WHO WAS HE?

He was a Shi'a Muslim cleric and political leader of the 1979 Iranian Revolution that overthrew Mohammad Reza Pahlavi, the last Shah of Iran.

## EARLY INFLUENCES

He was born into a family of Shi'ite scholars that claimed descent from Muhammad. His father was murdered when Ruhollah was five months old and he was raised by his extended family. In adulthood he changed his surname to that of his home town and became a theologian and teacher of Islamic law and was hailed as a religious leader (Ayatollah) in the 1950s.

He was exiled from Iran in 1964 for leading a religious movement against the Shah of Iran, and settled in the holy city of Najaf in Iraq where he became revered. Unlike the Shah he was anti-Israeli (believing the Jews were plotting to take over Iran) and anti-American. He opposed the Shah's "dangerous" secularization, which included land reforms, the enfranchisement of women, and a national anti-illiteracy campaign.

He returned in 1979 after the Shah had been deposed after huge street demonstrations and was named political and religious leader of the Islamic Republic of Iran for life.

## WHAT DID HE DO THAT WAS SO WRONG?

His regime was responsible for systematic human rights violations, including mass executions. As soon as he came to power he violently suppressed opposition, and set up a strict Islamic constitution based on Sharia (Islamic law). Women were forced to cover their hair and men were banned from wearing shorts or T-shirts. Alcohol and western music were banned. He called for Islamic revolutions across the Muslim world. This provoked Iraq, with the support of Saudi Arabia and the US, into the Iran-Iraq war which lasted for eight years, severely damaging the Iranian economy.

In 1989 he issued a fatwa against the British author Salman Rushdie, calling for his death, for committing blasphemy in his book *The Satanic Verses*.

## BODY COUNT

After the revolution thousands of members of the deposed regime were tortured and killed. Subsequently many university students were imprisoned without trial and killed for opposing the theocratic regime. In 1988 he issued an order that all political prisoners who did not repent their anti-regime conduct would be executed. In addition nearly a million Iranians were killed in the Iran-Iraq war.

## FAMOUS QUOTES

"The author of *The Satanic Verses* book, which is against Islam, the Prophet and the Koran, and all those involved in its publication who were aware of its content, are sentenced to death. I ask all Moslems to execute them wherever they find them."

# BÉLA KISS

**BIRTH NAME:** Béla Kiss
**TITLES:** "Hoffman" (alias)
**BIRTH:** 1877, Cinkota, Hungary
**DEATH:** unknown

## WHO WAS HE?

He was a Hungarian serial killer who murdered at least twenty-four young women and kept their corpses in giant metal drums.

## EARLY INFLUENCES

Little is known about his early life. As an adult he was a tinsmith who lived with his wife Marie. In 1912 he told neighbors that she had run off with another man, and after placing ads in the newspapers he began corresponding with available women, some of whom he invited to his home.

## WHAT DID HE DO THAT WAS SO WRONG?

When he was called up for the army in 1914 to fight in the First World War, he left his house heavily padlocked. It is unlikely that any of the villagers would have ventured out to his house anyway, since he had a reputation for being a sorcerer. Only one person, old Mrs. Jakubec, who did his cleaning, had even seen what he kept in the attic: seven large metal casks. She later swore that she knew nothing of their contents.

In 1916, while Kiss was still away fighting, the police broke into his house to investigate whether he was illegally hoarding petrol in his casks, which should have been used for the war effort. What they found was much worse. In each of the metal casks they discovered the decaying bodies of women who had been strangled. A search of the house uncovered many items of female clothing and jewelry, and when police dug up his garden they discovered another seventeen female bodies.

In a secret room in his house police found a library of books about poisoning and strangulation and correspondence with seventy-four women. Kiss had extorted money from many of them, and killed them if they became a nuisance. Two of his victims had started court proceeding against him before they "disappeared."

According to military records, Kiss died in a military hospital in Serbia. When police checked this information they discovered that the body was of a man many years younger than Kiss, who had swapped his identity tags and absconded; he was never brought to justice.

## BODY COUNT
Béla Kiss murdered at least twenty-four women, possibly including his own wife.

## FAMOUS QUOTES
"Please, sir, I know nothing of this terrible thing. I knew Béla Kiss only as a man who was kind to me and paid me well." (Mrs. Jakubec, housekeeper)

# ILSE KOCH

- **BIRTH NAME:** Ilse Köhler Schnitzel
- **TITLES:** "Witch of Buchenwald," "Bitch of Buchenwald"
- **BIRTH:** September 22, 1906, Dresden, Germany
- **DEATH:** September 1, 1967, hanged (suicide)

## WHO WAS SHE?

She was the wife of Karl Koch, the commandant of the concentration camp, Buchenwald.

## EARLY INFLUENCES

The daughter of a farmer, she was a polite and contented child who left school at the age of fifteen to work in a factory and then as a librarian. She joined the Nazi Party in 1932 and dated several SA soldiers. In 1936 she began working as a guard and secretary at the Sachsenhausen concentration camp near Berlin, where she met and married the commandant Karl Otto Koch. The following year they transferred to the newly built Buchenwald concentration camp where Isla's sadism was allowed full expression.

## WHAT DID SHE DO THAT WAS SO WRONG?

At Buchenwald she tortured inmates and selected many of them for execution. She used to ride her horse through the camp, whipping prisoners on a whim. One of her whips had razor blades at the end.

She used the tanned skin from murdered inmates to make lampshades, gloves, handbags, book covers, and gloves. Her dinner table was decorated with shrunken human heads.

In 1940 she built an indoor sports arena, which cost over 250,000 marks, using money confiscated from inmates. The following year she became an Oberaufseherin ("head supervisor") over twenty-two female guards who served at the camp.

In 1943 after her husband was arrested for embezzlement and removed from the camp, she struck up a relationship with the camp's doctor. In April 1945 as the allies advanced the camp was evacuated and Ilse live outside in quiet domestic comfort. She was arrested after many of the inmates informed US GIs about her sadism. She was charged with "participating in a common criminal plan for encouraging, aiding, abetting and participating in the atrocities at Buchenwald." She was found guilty and sentenced to life imprisonment, but committed suicide in Aichach women's prison in 1967.

## BODY COUNT

She was personally responsible for the deaths of scores of prisoners, as she hand-selected inmates with distinctive tattoos and earmarked them for extermination.

## FAMOUS QUOTES

"The finished products [i.e., tattooed skin detached from corpses] were turned over to Koch's wife, who had them fashioned into lampshades and other ornamental household articles . . ." (witness statement, Nuremburg Trials)

# RICHARD KUKLINSKI

- **BIRTH NAME:** Richard Kuklinski
- **TITLES:** "The Iceman"
- **BIRTH:** April 11, 1935, Jersey City, New Jersey, USA
- **DEATH:** March 5, 2006, natural causes

## WHO WAS HE?

He was a notorious hit man who was connected to the Gambino crime family.

## EARLY INFLUENCES

He grew up in a violent household, and was regularly beaten by both his alcoholic father and his mother. He tortured animals during his childhood, because he was curious about his lack of empathy. During his teens Kuklinski was bullied by street gangs until he fought back, beating six boys close to death with a stick. He said that this was a turning point in his life, because for the first time he felt in powerful and in control.

## WHAT DID HE DO THAT WAS SO WRONG?

When he was twenty-one he committed his first murder by fatally injuring a man with a snooker cue during a bar brawl (although he claimed to have murdered when he was fourteen).

He had an imposing physique, standing 6 feet 4 inches and weighing 300 pounds. He began doing robberies and running errands for the Gambino crime family and later became a hit man for them. He married and had children but his family remained blissfully ignorant of his real career.

He gained his nickname "The Iceman" because he often disguised the time of death of his victims by freezing their bodies before disposing of them. He often killed his victims by spraying them in the face with liquid cyanide as he walked past; they would be dead within twenty seconds.

He was completely dispassionate about killing, as shown by an incident involving a crossbow. He wanted to use it to make a hit, but he needed to try it out first, so he got into his car and then stopped a pedestrian to ask directions. When the man bent forward, he shot him in the forehead, and according Kuklinski the bolt "went half-way through his head."

Kuklinski was arrested after an undercover operation in 1986, when an FBI agent posed as a client hiring him for a hit. He was given two life sentences.

## BODY COUNT

Kuklinski killed regularly over a thirty-year period. An exact figure is impossible to verify, but Kuklinski claims to have made more than 200 kills.

## FAMOUS QUOTES

"I'm not the Iceman, I'm the Nice Man"

"Take off the cuffs. Take off the shackles. Let me run and shoot me in the back. Let's get it over with."

# OSAMA BIN LADEN

- **BIRTH NAME:** Osama bin Muhammed bin 'Awad bin Laden
- **TITLES:** (Aliases) "Usama bin Muhammad bin Ladin,"
"Shaykh Usama bin Ladin," "the Prince," "the Emir,"
"Abu Abdallah," "Al-Mujahid Shaykh," "Hajj," "the Director"
- **BIRTH:** March 10, 1957, Riyadh, Saudi Arabia
- **DEATH:** still alive (although newspapers have reported his death twice)

## WHO IS HE?

He is an Islamic fundamentalist and founding leader of the terrorist organization known as Al-Qaeda, "The Base." He is 6 foot 5 inches tall, left-handed, diabetic, and suffers with chronically low blood pressure.

## EARLY INFLUENCES

He is the seventeenth son of billionaire Saudi businessman, Muhammed bin Laden. He was educated at the Al-Thager Model School in Jeddah (a secular school with a Western-style uniform) and has a degree in economics and public administration from King Abdulaziz University.

Ironically, he is a monster of the USA's own making. During the Soviet-Afghan war (1979–88) he was supported by the CIA, to fight the Soviet invaders, and ran one of seven anti-Soviet militias there.

He founded Al Qaeda in 1988 to consolidate the international network he established during the Afghan war. Its mission was to advance Islamic revolutions throughout the Muslim world and to repel foreign intervention in the Middle East. Following the first Gulf War it shifted its focus to the expulsion of US troops from the Middle East and destruction of the State of Israel and the US. In the early 1990s the Saudi regime deported him and revoked his citizenship.

## WHAT DID HE DO THAT WAS SO WRONG?
He is wanted by the FBI in connection with the September 11, 2001, attack on the World Trade Centre and the Pentagon. He is also responsible for the August 7, 1998, bombings of the United States embassies in Dar es Salaam, Tanzania, and Nairobi, Kenya.

Former CIA Director George Tenet has stated that bin Laden has the capacity to plan "multiple attacks with little or no warning." The Rewards for Justice Program, United States Department of State, is offering a reward of up to $25 million for information leading directly to his apprehension or conviction. An additional reward of $2 million is being offered by the Airline Pilots Association and the Air Transport Association.

## BODY COUNT
At least 2,985 people were killed on 9/11 and over 200 people have been killed in other Al Qaeda attacks. Seventeen American servicemen were killed in October 2000 when Al Qaeda bombed the USS *Cole*, an American guided-missile destroyer at Aden, Yemen.

## FAMOUS QUOTES
"Hostility toward America is a religious duty, and we hope to be rewarded for it by God .... I am confident that Muslims will be able to end the legend of the so-called superpower that is America." (Time)

# MARC LÉPINE

- **BIRTH NAME:** Gamil Gharbi
- **TITLES:** "Montreal University Killer"
- **BIRTH:** October 26, 1964, Montreal, Canada
- **DEATH:** December 6, 1989, shot (suicide)

## WHO WAS HE?

He was a Canadian mass murderer who killed fourteen women in the "Ecole Polytechnique Massacre" in 1989.

## EARLY INFLUENCES

The son of an Algerian immigrant and a Canadian woman, Lépine grew up in a violent household. His father violently beat his wife and children regularly. Lépine was a loner and had never had a relationship with a woman. He applied to join the Canadian Armed Forces but was turned down. His application to study engineering at the Ecole Polytechnique de Montreal was also rejected. Spurned by women and the University, he decided to take revenge on both.

## WHAT DID HE DO THAT WAS SO WRONG?

At 5:00 P.M. on December 6, 1989, armed with a Ruger Mini-14 semi-automatic rifle, Mark Lépine walked into an engineering lecture at the Ecole Polytechnique de Montreal, where two students were giving a presentation. He walked to the front of the class and said, "Everyone stop everything." At first students thought he was pulling a classroom prank, but they realized he meant business when he fired a round into the ceiling, and ordered them to split into two groups: men and women. He let the men go, which left nine women in the room. Lépine announced that he was fighting feminism. One of the students tried to reason with him, saying that just because they were women didn't mean that they were all feminists. Lépine responded by executing all nine of them, one by one. Six women died instantly, the other three died later of their wounds.

Lépine left the classroom and rampaged around the university killing five more women. He finished off one victim by stabbing her three times in the chest. Then he took off his coat, wrapped it around the muzzle of his gun and shot himself in the head. Witnesses reported that the top part of his skull flew across the room. He left behind a three-page suicide note blaming feminists for destroying his life, and explaining the social changes in society that had led to his actions.

## BODY COUNT
Lépine killed fourteen women and injured thirteen others (four men and nine women).

## FAMOUS QUOTES
"Even though the Mad Killer epithet will be attributed to me by the media, I consider myself a rational and erudite person that only the arrival of the Grim Reaper has forced to undertake extreme acts. For why persevere in existing if it is only to please the government? Being rather retrograde by nature (except for science), the feminists always have a talent for enraging me. They want to retain the advantages of being women (e.g., cheaper insurance, extended maternity leave preceded by a preventive leave) while trying to grab those of the men." (extract of suicide note)

"Ah, shit." (last words)

# BOBBY JOE LONG

- **BIRTH NAME:** Robert Joe Long
- **TITLES:** "The Classified Ad Rapist"
- **BIRTH:** October 14, 1953, Kenova, West Virginia, USA
- **DEATH:** still alive

## WHO IS HE?
He is an American serial rapist and killer who operated in Florida between 1974 and 1984.

## EARLY INFLUENCES
Long was brought up by his overprotective mother after his father left and slept in his mother's bed until he was thirteen years old. He suffered a series of head injuries as a child: he was knocked unconscious after a fall from a swing at age five; was severely concussed when he crashed his bicycle a year later; and at age seven he fell off a pony and complained of dizziness and nausea for several days afterwards. He also suffered from Klinefelter's syndrome, which meant he had an extra X (female) chromosome and developed breasts during puberty.

## WHAT DID HE DO THAT WAS SO WRONG?
His deviant behavior appears to have been triggered by a fourth head injury sustained during a serious motorcycle accident in 1974 in which he almost lost a leg. Afterwards his sex drive increased so much that he needed to masturbate at least six times a day to find relief.

He raped scores of women over a ten-year period, and then killed nine women during a six-month killing spree. Between 1980 and 1983 he raped women in the Miami, Ocala, and Fort Lauderdale area by answering small ads placed by people selling household items, usually bedroom furniture. He would turn up at the woman's address when he knew that she would be home alone, on the pretext of inspecting the goods. He appeared well dressed and respectable. If she seemed to be alone he pulled a knife and forced his way in to the house, then tied his victim up, raped and robbed her. While he raped women he liked to make them talk to him.

He also preyed on hookers and hitchhikers, forcing them to strip naked and lie in the front seat of his car. He usually tied their hands behind their back and raped them, before driving them to another location where he would rape them a second time, often anally. He killed them by a mixture of strangling, beating, and stabbing. He killed so casually, that on one occasion he put his dinner in the oven, went to the corner store to get some milk, and killed a woman on his way back. After each murder, Long would go home and sleep deeply, then get up and read about the murder in the paper and convince himself that his latest victim was just another "slut" who deserved to die.

He was arrested in November 1984 and was given three death sentences.

## BODY COUNT
He raped between 25 and 150 women, some as young as twelve, and murdered nine women.

## FAMOUS QUOTES
"Give a bitch a choice between getting dicked and getting hurt, you know what she's gonna pick."

# PEDRO ALONSO LÓPEZ

- **BIRTH NAME:** Pedro Alonso López Monsalve
- **TITLES:** "Monster of the Andes"
- **BIRTH:** October 8, 1948, Santa Isabel, Colombia
- **DEATH:** still alive

## WHO IS HE?

He is a South American serial killer who murdered more than 350 children in Peru, Colombia, and Ecuador.

## EARLY INFLUENCES

He was the seventh son of a Colombian prostitute. He had twelve brothers and several sisters, one of whom he was caught molesting when he was eight years old, whereupon his mother kicked him out of the house and he became a street urchin. Almost immediately he was kidnapped by a pedophile who subjected him to days of sexual abuse, until he managed to escape. However, as a homeless child in Colombia, his childhood and adolescence were characterized by many similar incidents of rape and sodomy. When he was eighteen after being caught stealing a car, he was sent to prison where he was brutalized further.

## WHAT DID HE DO THAT WAS SO WRONG?

In prison he was gang raped by four men. Two weeks later he got his revenge by stabbing three of them to death. After years of abuse and living rough, the prison rape was the trigger for his killing spree. After his release from prison in 1978 he moved to Peru and started killing.

His modus operandi was to loiter around a public place such as a market until he spotted a young, innocent looking girl. He would follow her for several days, and finally when he could get her on his own he would give her a small gift, then take her somewhere else with the promise that he was going to fetch a present for her mother. He would take the child to a secret hideaway where he would cuddle her during the night and then rape her at sunrise and strangle her. He waited for daylight so he could see his victim's face while she died.

He buried his victims in graves nearby, but often he kept three or four corpses unburied so that he could have macabre tea parties with a group of dead playmates.

Early in his killing career his murders almost came to an abrupt end, when he was caught trying to abduct a nine-year-old girl from a tribe of Peruvian Indians. They brutally punished him by whipping and burning him, and was only spared execution when an American Christian missionary pleaded on his behalf. After much persuasion the Indians released him and López moved to Ecuador, where he continued raping and killing.

He was finally caught after a flash flood uncovered four murdered children. In custody he confessed to murdering over 300 victims and took police to the sites of at least fifty graves. He was sentenced to life in prison, but was released in 1998, despite vowing to kill again. His current whereabouts are unknown.

## BODY COUNT
He raped and murdered at least 350 children in three countries.

## FAMOUS QUOTES
"I am the man of the century. No one will ever forget me."

# HENRY LEE LUCAS & OTTIS TOOLE

- **BIRTH NAME:** Henry Lee Lucas
- **TITLES:** "Serial Killer"
- **BIRTH:** August 23, 1936, Blacksburg, Virginia, USA
- **DEATH:** March 13, 2001, heart attack

- **BIRTH NAME:** Ottis Elwood Toole
- **TITLES:** "Serial Killer and Cannibal"
- **BIRTH:** March 5, 1947, Jacksonville, Florida, USA
- **DEATH:** September 15, 1996, liver failure

## WHO WERE THEY?

They were an American serial killer and cannibal team operating in the late seventies and early eighties.

## EARLY INFLUENCES

Henry was born into a poor family with nine children, most of whom were brought up by relatives or in foster homes. Henry stayed at home, where his mother, a violent prostitute, repeatedly beat him, and forced him to watch her having sex. Once she hit him so hard with a plank of wood that he was in a coma for a day. Later, as a result of the beatings he started having seizures and hearing voices. He was often sent to school in a dress. His alcoholic father committed suicide. Henry was an alcoholic by the time he was ten, and during his adolescence he had sex with live and dead animals.

Ottis was abandoned by his father when he was young and his mother was a religious fanatic. He claimed that his sister dressed him in girl's clothes and that his grandmother was a satanist. He frequently ran away from home and was a fire starter who gained sexual pleasure from arson.

## WHAT DID THEY DO THAT WAS SO WRONG?

On January 11, 1960, Henry stabbed his mother to death and raped her corpse. He was sent to prison for forty years, but was released after only ten. A year later he tried to kidnap a young girl from a bus stop at gunpoint, and served another four years.

Ottis claimed to have committed his first murder at the age of fourteen, when he ran over a traveling salesman in his own car after the man had tried to molest him.

Ottis and Lucas met in a Jacksonville soup kitchen in 1978 and started picking up hitchhikers and killing them, in the words of Lucas, "every which way there is except one. I haven't poisoned anyone." Toole was a cannibal who liked to eat human flesh cooked in barbecue sauce. According to Lucas, he would have joined in the feast, but he didn't like barbecue sauce. However, he was partial to necrophilia.

Lucas started dating Toole's young niece Frieda Powell, but killed her after she slapped him during an argument, had sex with her corpse, then chopped up her body.

Lucas was arrested in June 15, 1983, for a minor weapons charge, and while in custody he confessed the murder of eighty-two-year-old Kate Rich one year earlier and Frieda Powell. In April 1984, Toole was convicted of a 1982 arson incident that killed sixty-four-year-old George Sonnenberg in Jacksonville, Florida.

## BODY COUNT

In prison both men confessed to hundreds of murders. Nobody knows how many people they really killed. Many investigators believe that the pair was responsible for at least fifty murders.

## FAMOUS QUOTES

"Killing someone is just like walking outdoors. If I wanted a victim I'd just go and get one." (Lucas)

"I killed people I didn't think was worth living anyhow." (Toole)

"I'm not some kind of saint, but I do believe I'll go to heaven." (Lucas)

# CHARLES MANSON

- ► **BIRTH NAME:** Charles Milles Maddox
- ► **TITLES:** "Mac," "Charlie"
- ► **BIRTH:** November 12, 1934, Cincinnati, Ohio, USA
- ► **DEATH:** still alive

## WHO IS HE?

He was a career criminal and an American cult leader of the Manson "Family," which committed several murders, known collectively as the Tate-LaBianca murders.

## EARLY INFLUENCES

He was born to a sixteen-year-old mother and never knew his father. When Manson was five, his mother and his uncle were convicted of sexual assault and for holding up a gas station. When he was thirteen his mother tried and failed to put him in a foster home, and sent him instead to a reform school in Indiana, from which he ran away and became a homeless petty criminal. By the time he was eighteen he had spent time in several juvenile facilities, had raped another boy, and had collected eight assault charges against him. This pattern continued, so that by 1969 when the Tate-LaBianca murders happened, Manson had already spent seventeen years in custody.

## WHAT DID HE DO THAT WAS SO WRONG?

Manson was the leader of the cult called the "Family." He developed a race war philosophy that blacks would rise up and take over American cities in a revolution which he called "Helter Skelter," a name taken from the Beatles' *White Album*. He believed that he was an angel and that he would reclaim Los Angeles and then enter the hidden city under Death Valley.

Using a combination of charisma, drugs, and brutality, he convinced his followers to murder Sharon Tate (the wife of movie director Roman Polanski) and six other people in Beverly Hills on August 9, 1969, and Leno and Rosemary LaBianca the following day in what became known as the Tate-LaBianca murders. Most of the victims were stabbed repeatedly and the words "Death to Pigs," "Helter Skelter [sic]" and "Rise" were written on the walls with their blood. The family also murdered a music teacher Gary Hinman and wrote "Political Piggy" on his wall.

If they had not been arrested, the Family intended to torture and murder several celebrities, including Frank Sinatra, Richard Burton, Elizabeth Taylor, and Tom Jones.

## BODY COUNT

The Manson "Family" killed nine people, including an eight-month-old baby in utero. Although Manson didn't commit any of the murders himself, they were performed at his bidding.

## FAMOUS QUOTES

"Look down at me and you see a fool; look up at me and you see a god; look straight at me and you see yourself."

"If I could get some help from the doctor then I could get my mind-straightened out a little bit and I come back and play like a human."

"Remorse for what? You people have done everything in the world to me. Doesn't that give me equal right?"

# PETER MANUEL

- **BIRTH NAME:** Peter Thomas Anthony Manuel
- **TITLES:** "Serial Killer"
- **BIRTH:** March 1, 1927, New York, USA
- **DEATH:** July 11, 1958, hanged (executed)

## WHO WAS HE?

He was a serial killer, born in the USA, who killed up to fifteen people in Scotland during the 1950s. He is considered one of the most psychopathic killers in British criminal history.

## EARLY INFLUENCES

Manuel was born to Scottish immigrants in the USA in 1927, who moved to Coventry, England, when he was five years old. He was arrested for burglary at the age of twelve and spent much of his adolescence in approved schools and borstal.

## WHAT DID HE DO THAT WAS SO WRONG?

At age sixteen he was jailed for sexual assault of a school employee, and served further sentences for rape during the next decade, before moving in 1956 to the village of Birkenshaw in North Lanarkshire, Scotland, where his parents were now living, and began his killing spree. His weapons were a Webley revolver, a Beretta pistol, and an iron bar.

In 1956 police questioned him for the murder of seventeen-year-old Anna Knielands, who had been attacked with an iron bar on the fifth fairway at East Kilbride Golf Course, but he was a convincing liar and was released without charge. In September of that year, forty-five-year-old Marion Watt, her sixteen-year-old daughter Vivienne, and Marion's sister Margaret were found dead at their home in Glasgow. They had been shot. Manuel was again questioned without charge, although he was jailed for eighteen months for a burglary.

After his release from prison Manuel shot dead a taxi driver in Newcastle Upon Tyne, then returned to Glasgow, where he killed four more people over Christmas 1957: seventeen-year-old Isabelle Cooke, whom he buried in a field, and a middle-aged Uddingston couple and their ten-year-old son. After the murder he snacked on their festive leftovers and fed the family cat. He was arrested two weeks later after using banknotes he had stolen from his last victims in a local pub.

Arrested on the January 14, 1958, he was charged with seven murders and conducted his own defense very competently at his trial at Glasgow High Court. He pleaded insanity without success and was sentenced to be hanged. Just before his execution in Barlinnie prison in Glasgow on July 11, 1958, he confessed to the murders plus several more with which the police had not previously linked him.

## BODY COUNT
Although he was found guilty of seven murders, he is believed to have killed up to fifteen people.

## FAMOUS QUOTES
"He displayed a brutality and viciousness that was truly shocking, even in 1950s Glasgow where gangland feuds, bungled robberies, and pub fights often ended in death." (Iain Lundy)

"Turn up the radio and I'll go quietly." (Last words)

# FERDINAND MARCOS

- **BIRTH NAME:** Ferdinand Emmanuel Edralín Marcos
- **TITLES:** "President of the Philippines"
- **BIRTH:** September 11, 1917, Sarrat, Philippines
- **DEATH:** September 28, 1989, kidney failure

## WHO WAS HE?

He was the tenth president of the Philippines, ruling from 1965 to 1986.

## EARLY INFLUENCES

The second of four children, his father was a lawyer and politician and his mother was a teacher. While studying Law at the University of the Philippines, he was sent to prison for murdering Congressman Julio Nalundasan, one of his father's political opponents. He appealed his sentence, and bribed his way to freedom. He collaborated with the Japanese during the Second World War, although his official biography claims that he was a war hero member of the Philippine resistance. Then he entered politics and became wealthy through gold dealing and taking bribes, and he switched political parties when it suited him. He became President in 1969.

## WHAT DID HE DO THAT WAS SO WRONG?

His first term in office was quite promising, but in 1972 he declared martial law, suspending the constitution to become effectively a dictator. He used the army to kill, torture, and imprison his political opponents.

His regime became the world's biggest kleptocracy. He gave his wife, Imelda, and members of his family top jobs (Imelda was Minister for Culture and Governor of Manila) and embezzled billions of dollars during his twenty-one years in office (some estimates are as high as $100 billion, making the Marcos family the richest in the world). While the population starved, they spent lavishly. On a single shopping trip to USA they spent $3.3 million. Marcos even used gold bricks to build partition walls in his house and Imelda famously owned over 4,000 pairs of shoes.

In 1981 he suspended martial law, but had his political opponent Benigno Aquino assassinated, shot dead as he stepped off the airplane after spending eight years in exile. Aquino's wife stood against Marcos in the subsequent election, and even though Marcos rigged the result and arrested yet more opponents, public rioting forced him out of the country (he was flown to safety in Hawaii by the CIA).

## BODY COUNT

During the Marcos years more than 3,000 opponents were murdered, 35,000 people tortured and 100,000 were imprisoned, while his pilfering forced his people to live in abject poverty.

## FAMOUS QUOTES

"There are many things we do not want about the world. Let us not just mourn them. Let us change them."

"It is easier to run a revolution than a government."

# TIMOTHY McVEIGH

- **BIRTH NAME:** Timothy James McVeigh
- **TITLES:** "Oklahoma City Bomber"
- **BIRTH:** April 23, 1968, Pendleton, New York, USA
- **DEATH:** June 11, 2001, lethal injection (executed)

## WHO WAS HE?

He was an American terrorist who carried out the Oklahoma City bombing on April 19, 1995, one of the worst cases of domestic terrorism in US history.

## EARLY INFLUENCES

His home community was incredulous when McVeigh was arrested for the bombing, because he had been an intelligent and good-natured child. His parents divorced when he was ten and he lived with his father. When he was twenty he joined the US Army and served in the Gulf War, where he was awarded a Bronze Star and was considered a model soldier, but he later claimed that he was shocked to be ordered to execute surrendering prisoners. After failing to get into the elite Green Berets, he left the army in December 1991. He became a security guard, experimented with methamphetamines and became disaffected, a forgotten "war hero" in search of an identity and a new purpose in life.

## WHAT DID HE DO THAT WAS SO WRONG?

On April 19, 1995, he parked a yellow Ryder Rental truck filled with 5,000 pounds of homemade explosive outside the Alfred P. Murrah Federal Building. The bomb exploded at 9:02 A.M. and the north half of the building collapsed with devastating injury and loss of life, as well as damage to 300 other buildings.

The date of the explosion was the two-year anniversary of the storming of the Branch-Davidian complex in Waco, Texas, by the FBI, which resulted in the death of seventy-six Branch-Davidian members. McVeigh believed that the act constituted wide-scale mass murder on the part of the US government, and so, inexplicably, the bombing was his way of defending the Constitution and punishing the government by creating an atrocity of his own.

The FBI tracked the serial number on the rear axle of the rented van to McVeigh and he was quickly apprehended.

## BODY COUNT

The bomb killed 168 people, including 19 children in a day-care center located on the ground floor of the building, and injured 850 others.

## FAMOUS QUOTES

"Based on observations of the policies of my own government, I viewed this action as an acceptable option."

"If I had known there was an entire day-care center, it might have given me pause to switch targets. That's a large amount of collateral damage."

"I am sorry these people had to lose their lives. But that's the nature of the beast. It's understood going in what the human toll will be."

# CATHERINE DE' MEDICI

- **BIRTH NAME:** Caterina Maria Romola di Lorenzo de' Medici
- **TITLES:** "Queen of France"
- **BIRTH:** April 13, 1519, Florence, Italy
- **DEATH:** January 5, 1589, pneumonia

## WHO WAS SHE?

She was the Queen of France as the wife of King Henri II of France, and became Regent after his death.

## EARLY INFLUENCES

She was the daughter of Lorenzo II de' Medici, Duke of Urbino and a French princess, Madeleine de la Tour d'Auvergne, both of whom died when she was a baby. She was educated in a convent and married the Duke of Orléans when she was fourteen; he later became King Henry II of France. She was attractive, intelligent, and ruthless.

## WHAT DID SHE DO THAT WAS SO WRONG?

She was responsible for the St. Bartholomew's Day massacre in which thousands of Huguenots were slaughtered in Paris; it began on August 24, 1572, and lasted for several days. She convinced her son King Charles IX that the Protestant Huguenots were plotting to overthrow the Catholic monarchy, so he reluctantly ordered a death squad of 1,200 soldiers to commit wholesale slaughter of innocent men, women, and children.

The city gates were closed on the evening of August 23, and the doors of Huguenot houses were painted with a cross. At 2:00 A.M. the following morning the killing began. Huguenots were dragged into the street where they were beaten to death and stabbed with swords. Babies were thrown into the Seine and used for target practice. Soon the violence spread against anyone wealthy and looting and killing grew out of control. When Charles saw the scale of the killing he ordered it to stop, but it was too late. The Seine was soon filled with floating corpses.

After the massacre Catherine tried to pass off the slaughter as a breakdown in communication, claiming she had only intended for a handful of Huguenots to be killed. Meanwhile, Pope Gregory XIII minted a medal to celebrate the occasion.

Catherine also assassinated many of her rivals by poisoning and had a hidden trap door to dispose of the bodies.

## BODY COUNT

Estimates of those killed range from 4,000 to 10,000, but many more were injured and robbed.

## FAMOUS QUOTES

"Kill them all, every one of them! Do not leave a single Huguenot to reproach me!"

# JOSEF MENGELE

- **BIRTH NAME:** Josef Mengele
- **TITLES:** "Angel of Death"
- **BIRTH:** March 16, 1911, Günzburg, Germany
- **DEATH:** February 7, 1979, drowned after a stroke

## WHO WAS HE?

He was a high-ranking Nazi SS officer and a physician in the concentration camp Auschwitz-Birkenau.

## EARLY INFLUENCES

He was the eldest of three sons, born to a wealthy industrialist. He studied veterinary medicine and anthropology at the University of Munich and then gained a PhD with a thesis on racial differences. He joined the Nazi party in 1937 and the SS the following year. At the beginning of the Second World War he served in the reserve medical corps and a Waffen-SS unit, and then was promoted to SS-Hauptsturmführer (Captain) after being wounded on the Russian front. In 1943 he became medical officer of Auschwitz-Birkenau.

## WHAT DID HE DO THAT WAS SO WRONG?

When the trains arrived at Auschwitz, he supervised the selection of which prisoners would be sent to the gas chambers, which would become prisoners, and which would enter his laboratory for medical experimentation.

In his genetic search for a superrace, Mengele performed horrific experiments on thousands of prisoners, especially his pet subjects: twins, gypsies, dwarfs, and children. He performed coldwater immersion experiments in which many prisoners froze to death; he sewed identical twins together back to back and at the wrists to make them artificially conjoined; he administered huge doses of X-rays to cause sterilization; he pressed the stomachs of pregnant women with weights to cause miscarriage; and he killed many simply so he could dissect them.

In 1945 he was captured by the Allies and held as a POW near Nuremburg, but he was released as his true identity was unknown. He then fled to South America living in Argentina, Paraguay, and Brazil and was never brought to justice for his crimes against humanity.

## BODY COUNT

At Auschwitz-Birkenau 1.1 million Jews, 75,000 Poles, and some 19,000 Roma (gypsies) were killed. He was personally responsible for the senseless torture and deaths of thousands of prisoners.

## FAMOUS QUOTES

"My friend! It will go on, and on, and on." (His reply to the question, "When will all this extermination cease?")

# SLOBODAN MILOŠEVIĆ

- **BIRTH NAME:** Slobodan Milošević
- **TITLES:** "President of Serbia," "President of Yugoslavia"
- **BIRTH:** August 20, 1941, Požarevac (today in Serbia)
- **DEATH:** March 11, 2006, heart attack

## WHO WAS HE?

He was President of Serbia from 1989 to 1997 and of Yugoslavia from 1989 to 2000.

## EARLY INFLUENCES

Milošević's parents separated soon after he was born and he was brought up by his mother, a straight-laced schoolteacher and member of the Communist Party. She boasted that one day her son would be a great leader. When he was twenty-one his father, a deacon in the Serbian Orthodox Church, committed suicide, and his mother hanged herself twelve years later.

He went on to study law at Belgrade University, climbed up the Communist Party hierarchy, and by 1986 he was the head of the Serbian Communist Party. Three years later he became President of Serbia by championing the grievances of the Serbian minority in Kosovo, who were protesting against harassment from the Albanian majority. In 1987, he famously announced, in response to a Serb protester who complained of being beaten by the police, "You will not be beaten." For many people this provocative statement marked the end of Yugoslavia, and became a rallying call for Serb nationalists. Milošević warned that if Yugoslavia should break up, Serbia's boundaries would need to be redrawn.

## WHAT DID HE DO THAT WAS SO WRONG?

Milošević's reawakening of Serbian nationalism and his policy of establishing "all Serbs in one state" led to a civil war in 1991 that lasted for four years. By December, 1991, Serbs had taken control of nearly a third of Croatia's territory, with 20,000 killed and half a million made homeless. In 1992 violence broke out in Bosnia and Herzegovina, and Serb forces soon captured about two-thirds of the country, and hundreds of thousands of Serbs and non-Serbs were displaced from the homes, and many thousands were killed in ethnic cleansing atrocities such as those at Srebrenica and Bratunac where approximately 11,000 Bosnian men and boys were executed by the Bosnian Serb Army.

In August 1995, Croatia drove out the remaining 200,000 Serbs from their self-proclaimed Republic of Serbian Krajina, and negotiations in Dayton, Ohio, brought temporary peace. The now unpopular Milošević brutally suppressed anti-government protests in 1996–7 and his cronies in the federal parliament elected him president of Yugoslavia. Then he started fresh conflict in an attempt to drive the Muslim majority out of Kosovo. NATO launched a bombing campaign which lasted seventy-eight days and reduced Serbia to ruins. Then Milošević tried to rebrand himself as the rebuilder of Serbia, but when he refused to recognize his defeat in an election, there were more mass protests, and in October he stepped down.

In June 2001 Milošević was handed over to The Hague tribunal for crimes against humanity. He died of a heart attack weeks before the conclusion of his trial.

## BODY COUNT
Milošević was indicted for crimes against humanity including systematic ethnic cleansing. Tens of thousands of people lost their lives, and hundreds of thousands were displaced in the bloodiest fighting in Europe since the Second World War.

## FAMOUS QUOTES
"You will not be beaten."

"It is difficult to say today whether the Battle of Kosovo was a defeat or a victory for the Serbian people, whether thanks to it we fell into slavery or we survived in this slavery."

"The truth can not be drowned by any flood of false indictments."

# HERMAN WEBSTER MUDGETT

- **BIRTH NAME:** Herman Webster Mudgett
- **TITLES:** "Dr. H. H. Holmes"
- **BIRTH:** May 16, 1861, Gilmantown, New Hampshire, USA
- **DEATH:** May 7, 1896, hanged (executed)

## WHO WAS HE?

He was the first identified serial killer in the United States; he killed scores of people in a specially built "torture castle" that he opened as a hotel for the World's Columbian Exposition in 1893.

## EARLY INFLUENCES

He grew up in a poor family, with an alcoholic abusive father. Unpopular at school, he was relentlessly bullied by neighborhood kids. He dissected live animals and dreamed of being a doctor. He briefly attended Michigan Medical School, but was expelled for his bizarre behavior, which included an incident involving a female corpse. He set up as a pharmacist in Chicago, under the alias Dr. H. H. Holmes, and began his life of crime.

## WHAT DID HE DO THAT WAS SO WRONG?

His early crimes involved fraud, forgery, real estate and insurance scams, and bigamy. Then he spotted a vacant lot across the road from his pharmacy. He built a three-story building on it, which neighbors christened "The Castle." He rented out the bottom floor for shops, but the upper floors were a maze of windowless soundproofed rooms with secret doors, false floors, trapdoors, peepholes, sliding walls, and other devices intended to control his victims. He opened it as a hotel for the World's Columbian Exposition in 1893 and then over the next three years he lured women, a mixture of his customers, lovers, and employees, into his maze. Here he raped, tortured and killed them with impunity. He had even designed a pipe system so that he could pump poisonous gas into any room of his choice.

None of the builders whom he had hired to build the place guessed his sinister intentions because he constantly sacked them and employed new ones. He disposed of the bodies by sending them down a special chute leading to the basement, where he stripped the flesh off the bones in vats of acid, burnt the victims' flesh in a huge furnace and sold the skeletons and some of the organs for medical science. He even placed some of his victims on an "elasticity determinator" to see how far the human body could stretch.

## BODY COUNT

Although Holmes only confessed to 27 murders, nine of which have been confirmed, it is likely that he killed as many as 230 victims, including his children and three wives.

## FAMOUS QUOTES

"I was born with the devil in me. I couldn't help the fact that I was a murderer, no more than a poet can help the inspiration to sing."

# ROBERT MUGABE

- **BIRTH NAME:** Robert Mugabe
- **TITLES:** "President of Zimbabwe"
- **BIRTH:** February 21, 1924, Rhodesia (Zimbabwe)
- **DEATH:** still alive

## WHO IS HE?

He has been the dictator of Zimbabwe since 1980, first as Prime Minister and from 1987 as the first executive President.

## EARLY INFLUENCES

He was raised in the Kutama Mission, Zvimba District, north-west of Harare, when the country was called Southern Rhodesia. He was educated in Roman Catholic Jesuit schools and qualified as a teacher at age seventeen. He became a Marxist and helped form the Zimbabwe African National Union (ZANU) which fought for Rhodesia's, ultimately Zimbabwe's, independence.

He and other nationalist leaders were imprisoned for ten years in 1964. After his release he went to Mozambique and with help from China his ZANU army, the Zimbabwe African National Liberation Army (ZANLA) conducted a guerrilla war against Ian Smith's whites-only government.

Ian Smith was forced to recognize that white minority rule could not continue. In 1979 talks on majority rule took place in London and elections were held in 1980. ZANU won the election and Mugabe became Prime Minister.

## WHAT DID HE DO THAT WAS SO WRONG?

At first Mugabe attempted to form a coalition between his northern homeland and his major rivals, the Zimbabwe African People's Union (ZAPU) from the South of the country, but this collapsed and fierce fighting broke out between ZANU and ZAPU supporters; Mugabe used the army to violently suppress opposition, and committed mass murder during this time.

In 1987 he restructured the country, turning it from a parliamentary democracy into a one-party state, with himself as President. He was re-elected for three consecutive terms, by rigging elections and intimidating his people. The economy began to collapse as the white middle classes left the country; those who remained had their farms forcibly seized and redistributed to blacks, many of whom were Mugabe's family and cronies. Much of this land now lies barren, creating famine where before there was agricultural plenty. Inflation has escalated to become the highest rate in the world.

His regime has systematically committed human rights abuses, persecuting homosexuals, restricting civil liberties, and torturing and assassinating opponents.

## BODY COUNT

Apart from the many thousands who have been persecuted and tortured, Mugabe was involved in the massacre of up to 20,000 people in Matabeleland during the 1980s. Zimbabweans now have the shortest life expectancy worldwide, listed as thirty-seven years for men, and thirty-four years for women.

## FAMOUS QUOTES

"The only white man you can trust is a dead white man."

"We don't mind having sanctions banning us from Europe. We are not Europeans."

"We are not hungry . . . Why foist this food upon us? We don't want to be choked. We have enough."

# HERBERT MULLIN

- **BIRTH NAME:** Herbert Williams Mullin
- **TITLES:** "Serial Killer"
- **BIRTH:** April 18, 1947, Santa Cruz, California, USA
- **DEATH:** still alive

## WHO IS HE?

He is a serial killer who operated in California in the early 1970s.

## EARLY INFLUENCES

He was a gentle and bright child, and grew up in a normal family. At school he was successful both academically and at sports; he was popular, played varsity football, and had no shortage of girlfriends. His classmates even voted him "most likely to succeed."

## WHAT DID HE DO THAT WAS SO WRONG?

After his best friend Dean Richardson was killed in a car crash the summer after high school graduation, Herbert's mental health began to deteriorate. He built a shrine to his dead friend in his bedroom and spent hours there grieving alone.

He dropped out of college and started experimenting with hallucinogenic drugs. Soon afterwards he was committed to a mental hospital exhibiting symptoms of schizophrenia. After his release he started hearing voices instructing him to kill. He obeyed them for the first time in October 1972, by pretending he had broken down on a deserted road in the Santa Cruz Mountains, and when a passerby stopped to help he bludgeoned him to death with a baseball bat. Two weeks later he fatally stabbed and eviscerated a college student, and a week later he stabbed a Catholic priest to death during confessional.

During the next three months, after a further ten murders, including five on the same day, he was arrested, and claimed that he had felt compelled to murder in order to prevent a devastating earthquake (his birthday was the anniversary of the 1906 San Francisco Earthquake). He also blamed his father: "Father was a Marine Corps sergeant and was used to ordering people to kill, I feel I was under my father's control, like a robot." He had often heard his father's voice "telepathically" instructing him to kill.

He is currently held at San Quentin and is scheduled for parole on the year 2025.

## BODY COUNT
He killed thirteen people in the space of four months.

## FAMOUS QUOTES
"One man consenting to be murdered protects the millions of other human beings living in the cataclysmic earthquake/tidal area. For this reason, the designated hero/leader and associates have the responsibilities of getting enough people to commit suicide and/or consent to being murdered every day."

"Every homo sapien communicates by mental telepathy . . . it's just not accepted socially."

# BENITO MUSSOLINI

- **BIRTH NAME:** Benito Amilcare Andrea Mussolini
- **TITLES:** "Il Duce"
- **BIRTH:** July 29, 1883, Predappio, Italy
- **DEATH:** April 28, 1945, firing squad (executed)

## WHO WAS HE?

He was the Fascist dictator of Italy from 1922 until his overthrow in 1943; he was a close ally of German dictator, Adolf Hitler.

## EARLY INFLUENCES

He was born into a working-class family; his father was a blacksmith and his mother a schoolteacher. He was a rowdy and disruptive child, and was twice expelled from school for violence against other classmates. In his teens and twenties he was a journalist for several Socialist newspapers and he developed his ideology of Fascism, with the aim of restoring Italy to the glory days of the Roman Empire. He fought in the First World War and was wounded out in 1917. After the war he organized his followers into a group of racists and violent thugs called Blackshirts, who took violent action against political opponents, persecuting socialists and unionists, breaking up strikes and attacking local government members.

## WHAT DID HE DO THAT WAS SO WRONG?

On October 28, 1922, his Blackshirts marched on Rome and toppled the government. Mussolini assumed dictatorial powers and then brutally suppressed all opposition. He replaced the king's guard with his own fascisti and set up the secret police force called the Ovra.

In 1924 he held rigged elections, and when the Socialist leader Giacomo Matteotti objected he had him murdered. Mussolini then made Italy a one-party state, banned trade unions, and killed political opponents.

In 1935 Mussolini invaded Ethiopia, gassed and bombed its inhabitants, entered into pact with Adolf Hitler known as the Axis, and supported Franco in Spain. In April 1939 he invaded Albania and fought on Hitler's side during the Second World War. When Sicily was captured by the allies in July 1943, Mussolini was imprisoned, but was rescued by a German SS Commando raid, and Hitler enabled him to set up a new Fascist state in northern Italy, where he ruled with even more brutality than before. Since 1938 he also persecuted Italian Jews, in line with Hitler's racial policies.

## BODY COUNT

Over 400,000 Italians were killed during the Second World War and he killed at least 30,000 Ethiopians during the Italian occupation of Ethiopia.

## FAMOUS QUOTES

"The eighteenth and nineteenth centuries experimented with democracy. The twentieth century will be the century of Fascism."

"Everybody dies the death that corresponds to his character."

# NERO

- **BIRTH NAME:** Lucius Domitius Ahenobarbus
- **TITLES:** "Emperor of the Roman Empire"
- **BIRTH:** December 15, 37, Antium, Italy
- **DEATH:** June 9, 68, suicide

## WHO WAS HE?

He was the fifth and last Roman Emperor of the Julio-Claudian dynasty.

## EARLY INFLUENCES

Nero was the only son of Gnaeus Domitius Ahenobarbus, a cruel and violent member of Caligula's staff who died when Nero was three year old. His mother was Agrippina the Younger, Caligula's sister. Nero was an active and intelligent child, but when his mother was banished from Rome by Caligula, Nero was cared for by his aunt Lepida, with whom he lived in relative poverty and neglect. After Caligula's death, he once again lived with his mother in luxury and was spoiled. He became emperor after the death of Claudius in 54, who, as some ancient historians believe, was poisoned by Nero's mother.

## WHAT DID HE DO THAT WAS SO WRONG?

When he was twenty-one he had his mother murdered, so that he could divorce his wife Octavia on grounds of infertility, leaving him free to marry Poppaea Sabina, the wife of a friend. Sometime later he kicked his now pregnant wife, Poppae to death in a violent rage.

On July 18, A.D. 64, the Great Fire of Rome started and raged for five days, destroying four of fourteen Roman districts and severely damaging seven. After the fire Nero built himself an enormous pleasure palace on the cleared ground. Roman historian Suetonius blamed Nero for starting the fire and singing while the city burned (the fiddle of popular mythology had not been invented yet). Nero blamed the fire on the Christians and used it as an excuse to torture thousands of them. Tacitus describes how "their deaths were made objects of amusement; dressed in the skins of wild animals they were torn to pieces by dogs, or crucified or burned alive, being used as torches when daylight ended. Nero provided his gardens for the spectacle burning Christians were used to proved lighting for chariot races. The human torches were stripped naked, rolled in tar, and then impaled on a spear and lit. Christian women and children weren't spared; Nero had them thrown to the lions in the Colosseum.

## BODY COUNT

Thousands of Christians and other enemies of the state died agonizing deaths during Nero's reign.

## FAMOUS QUOTES

"What an artist dies in me!" (Last words)

# CHARLES NG & LEONARD LAKE

- **BIRTH NAME:** Charles Chi-tat Ng
- **TITLES:** "Serial Killer"
- **BIRTH:** December 24, 1960, Hong Kong
- **DEATH:** still alive

**BIRTH NAME:** Leonard Lake

**TITLES:** "Serial Killer"

**BIRTH:** October 29, 1945, San Francisco, USA

**DEATH:** June 6, 1985, suicide (cyanide pills)

## WHO WERE THEY?

They were a pair of serial killers operating in North California during the 1980s.

## EARLY INFLUENCES

Lake was a bright child but he was obsessed with pornography from an early age, and took nude photos of his sister. He joined the Marines when he was twenty and served in Vietnam, but was discharged with medical illness. He was briefly married twice, but his wives left him after discovering that he had been appearing in hard core amateur porn movies. He was arrested in 1982 on a firearms charge, skipped bail and ended up at a remote cabin belonging to his in-laws in Wilseyville, where he was joined by Ng.

Ng was the son of a wealthy Hong Kong businessman. After being expelled from several schools, he was sent to a public school in Yorkshire, but was again expelled for stealing. He later spent a semester at a US college, but dropped out. In 1979 he was convicted of a hit-and-run accident, after which he joined the Marines (by lying about his birthplace). He was arrested for stealing military weapons from an armory at Kaneohe Marine Base in Hawaii, but escaped and met up with Lake at Wilseyville.

## WHAT DID THEY DO THAT WAS SO WRONG?

Police believe their killing spree began in July 1984. In a concrete bunker next to at the Wilseyville property, the pair tortured, raped, and murdered as many as twenty-five victims and recorded their deeds with a video camera. They burned some of the bodies in an incinerator, and buried others.

The men were survivalists who believed that nuclear war was imminent; they planned to survive in the bunker, and repopulate the planet with their stash of weapons and a harem of female slaves.

As soon as Lake was arrested he committed suicide by swallowing two cyanide pills taped to his lapel. Ng received the death sentence and is still appealing.

## BODY COUNT
The authorities identified the bodies of seven men, three women, two baby boys and recovered forty-five pounds of bone fragments. The evedence shows victims ranged in age from two to forty, but they believe that Lake and Ng murdered as many as twenty-five people including two entire families.

## FAMOUS QUOTES
"The perfect woman is totally controlled." (Lake)

"You can cry and stuff like the rest of them, but it won't do you no good. We are pretty, ha, cold-hearted." (Ng)

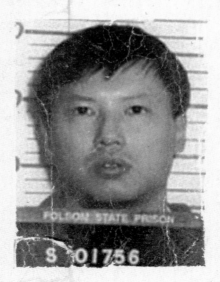

# DENIS NILSEN

- **BIRTH NAME:** Dennis Andrew Nilsen
- **TITLES:** "The British Jeffrey Dahmer"
- **BIRTH:** November 23, 1945, Strichen, Scotland, UK
- **DEATH:** still alive

## WHO IS HE?

He is a British serial killer and necrophiliac who stored corpses under his floorboards and in cupboards.

## EARLY INFLUENCES

Nilsen grew up in an unhappy household, the only child of parents who argued violently, and an alcoholic father who was often away from home. Nilsen claims he suffered two traumas during his childhood; the first was seeing the corpse of his grandfather when he was six years old, and the second was when he nearly drowned, and was rescued by an older boy who then sexually molested him.

In 1961, he became a cook in the Army Catering Corps, where he learned butchering, and in 1972 he spent a year as a trainee policeman, and was fascinated to observe autopsied bodies in the morgue. At home he enacted morbid fantasies by involving false blood and mirrors. He had several transient relationships, but he became deeply unhappy and lonely and late in 1978 he started killing men so that they could never leave him.

## WHAT DID HE DO THAT WAS SO WRONG?

Nilsen brought home gay men to his flat in Muswell Hill, North London, where he strangled them and kept the bodies for weeks, bathing and dressing the corpses in fresh pajamas, and having sex with them. He gathered so many rotting corpses in his bedroom that he had to keep spraying fly spray and air freshener.

He kept bodies underneath his floorboards, and then cut them up and burned them in his garden. The children who lived next door would watch his bonfires with excitement, unaware of their gruesome function. When the police arrested him they found over 1,000 human bone fragments in his garden. He decapitated his victims post mortem and boiled the heads on his kitchen stove to remove the flesh.

Nilsen was arrested on February 8, 1983, after body parts he had flushed down his toilet blocked the sewer pipe outside. The plumber who came to fix the problem became suspicious after he found several pieces of flesh in the sewer. That night neighbors spotted Nilsen trying to clean out the sewer, and the next day he was arrested.

He was sentenced to life imprisonment and will be eligible for parole in 2008.

## BODY COUNT

Nilsen killed and dismembered at least fifteen men between 1978 and 1983.

## FAMOUS QUOTES

"Loneliness is a long unbearable pain."

"I seek company first, and hope everything will be all right."

"If I'm not in tomorrow, I'll either be ill, dead, or in jail." (Said to a co-worker the evening before his arrest)

# ANTE PAVELIĆ

- **BIRTH NAME:** Ante Pavelić
- **TITLES:** "Butcher of the Balkans," "Poglavnik" (Chieftain)
- **BIRTH:** July 14, 1889, Bradina, Bosnia-Herzegovina
- **DEATH:** December 28, 1959, complications of his wounds following an assassination attempt two years earlier

## WHO WAS HE?

He was the leader of the Croatian fascist Ustaše movement during the 1930s and during the Second World War he was leader of the Independent State of Croatia, a puppet state of Nazi Germany.

## EARLY INFLUENCES

He attended primary school at Travnik in Bosnia-Herzegovina, received his secondary education in a Jesuit seminary in Senj, Croatia, and then he studied law at the University of Zagreb. He was a n extremist even in his youth, and joined the Croat Party of Rights (Hrvatska Stranka Prava, HSP), an extreme, right-wing nationalist group advocating Croat separatism. His avowed enemies were the Serbian Government, international Freemasonry, Jews, and communism.

## WHAT DID HE DO THAT WAS SO WRONG?

In 1929 he fled abroad after the establishment of the government of Alexander I of Yugoslavia, and formed the Ustaše terrorist organization. Terrorist training camps were set up in Italy and Hungary, where he received protection and financial support from Mussolini. The organization attempted an unsuccessful armed insurrection in 1933, and subsequently assassinated King Alexander I in October 1934.

When the Second World War broke out Paveli returned to Zagreb and became the leader of the Independent State of Croatia, a puppet state of Nazi Germany. He immediately declared the primary aim of his government as the "purification" of Croatia and the elimination of "alien elements." This "ethnic cleansing" involved the deportation of two million Serbs, Jews, and Gypsies and the deaths of hundreds of thousands. There are many documented cases of atrocities committed by the Ustaše, and in some cases Nazi officers even stepped in to stop the bloodshed, which included the widespread practice of gouging out eyes, and tying live victims in barbed wire and throwing them into mass graves. He is reputed to have kept a barrel full of human eyeballs next to his desk.

After the war he fled to Rome, where he was hidden by the Roman Catholic Church, then moved to Argentina, where he became Juan Peron's security advisor.

## BODY COUNT
The Ustaše was responsible for the deaths up to 30,000 Jews, up to 29,000 Gypsies, and 750,000 Serbs.

In September 1941 an Ustaše-run concentration camp was opened at Jasenovac, on the Bosnia-Herzegovina border southeast of Zagreb. Up to 200,000 people died there.

## FAMOUS QUOTES
"Kill a third, expel a third, and convert a third."

# AUGUSTO PINOCHET

- **BIRTH NAME:** Augusto José Ramón Pinochet Ugarte
- **TITLES:** "Dictator," "Grand Pa"
- **BIRTH:** November 25, 1915, Valparaíso, Chile
- **DEATH:** December 10, 2006, heart complications

## WHO WAS HE?

He was the head of the Chilean military junta that brutally tortured and killed thousands of Chileans during its 1973 to 1990 rule.

## EARLY INFLUENCES

Pinochet was born into an upper-middle-class Catholic family and his father was a customs official. At the age of eighteen he entered the military academy in Santiago, graduating three years later as a second lieutenant in the infantry in 1937. In 1943 he married Lucia Hiriart Rodriguez, with whom he fathered five children. He rose through the ranks, spending time as a teacher at the Military School as a professor of the War Academy in Arica. By 1973 Allende had appointed him Army Commander in Chief. Allende trusted Pinochet because he believed he lacked political ambition.

## WHAT DID HE DO THAT WAS SO WRONG?

On September 11, 1973, with CIA backing and funding, Pinochet seized power in Chile by overthrowing the democratically elected Communist leader, Salvatore Allende. He then immediately disbanded the country's legislature and established himself as dictator. In October 1973, at least seventy people were killed by the Caravan of Death, a Chilean Army squad that flew from prison to prison around Chile by helicopter, executing specific political targets.

Although he introduced a free-market economy and lowered inflation, Pinochet's legacy was one of torture, murder, and mayhem. His military police were responsible for the brutal torture of thousands of alleged dissidents and anyone who was even suspected of anti-government activities. According to Amnesty International, during his first year in power his regime tortured 180,000 people. Pinochet also embezzled and secreted millions in state money in various countries.

Amnesty has also detailed the torture methods that his regime used, including raping, electrocution, smashing bones, burning and removal of body parts. Victims were often decapitated after death to hamper identification, and the regime denied any involvement in the disappearances.

Pinochet visited Britain in 1998 for medical treatment, where he was arrested on charges of crimes against humanity and deported to Chile for trial, where he was eventually excused from trial for medical reasons.

## BODY COUNT
His regime resulted in the execution of over 3,000 Chilean residents, and the torture, imprisonment, and exile of tens of thousands.

## FAMOUS QUOTES
"I am a man who does not carry any hate in his heart. I don't want future generations to think badly of me."

"I'm not a dictator. It's just that I have a grumpy face."

"Sometimes democracy must be bathed in blood."

# POL POT

- **BIRTH NAME:** Saloth Sar
- **TITLES:** "Brother Number One," "Prime Minster of Cambodia"
- **BIRTH:** May 19, 1925, Prek Sbauv, Cambodia
- **DEATH:** April 15, 1998, heart failure

## WHO WAS HE?

He was the ruler of the Khmer Rouge and the Prime Minister of Cambodia from 1976 to 1979.

## EARLY INFLUENCES

Pol Pot was born into a wealthy family in Kampong Thum Province. He attended a Catholic school in Phnom Penh, and often visited the royal palace, because his sister was one of the king's concubines. He wasn't a promising student, so after moving to a technical school he continued his education in France. There he became involved with the French Communist movement (PCF) and joined a secret communist cell called the Cercle Marxiste where he quickly assumed a leadership role.

He returned to Cambodia in 1953 and spent the next decade in underground rebellion against the Cambodian government. In July 1962 he became the leader of the Communist party and fled to the Vietnamese border region where he developed the ideology and infrastructure of the Khmer Rouge, which grew rapidly. Pol Pot launched an uprising in 1968. Vietnam joined in and trained the Khmer Rouge, and China funded them with $5 million of weapons each year. By 1973 the Khmer Rouge controlled nearly two-thirds of the country, and in April 1975 it captured Phnom Penh.

## WHAT DID HE DO THAT WAS SO WRONG?

Khmer Rouge ideology considered the rural peasantry to be the real working class (despite the fact that the leaders were not drawn from this group). After taking control of the country it purged a quarter of the population, targeting intellectuals (anyone who seemed intelligent, e.g., people who wore glasses), ex-government officials and politicians, bureaucrats, Buddhists, the disabled, and minorities such as the Laotians and Vietnamese.

Mass evacuations of the cities were organized, in order to bring about a temporary return to a completely agrarian society, with the abandonment of technology. Hundreds of thousands of "bourgeois enemies" were forced into the countryside, to the "Killing Fields," where they had to dig their own mass graves before being beaten to death, or buried alive.

In 1979, Pol Pot led Cambodia into a disastrous war with Vietnam which caused the collapse of the Khmer Rouge government.

## BODY COUNT

Amnesty International estimated that 1.4 million people were killed during the purges, and thousands more in the war with Vietnam.

## FAMOUS QUOTES

"I did not join the resistance movement to kill people, to kill the nation. Look at me now. Am I a savage person? My conscience is clear."

"Since he is of no use anymore, there is no gain if he lives and no loss if he dies."

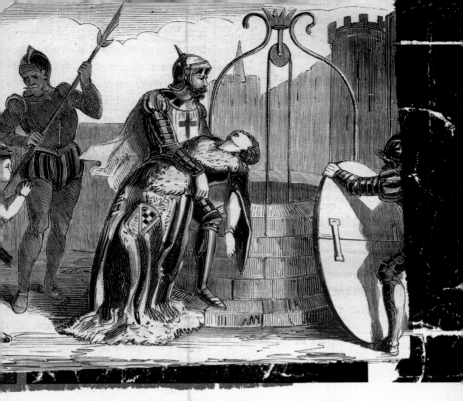

# GILLES DE RAIS

- **BIRTH NAME:** Gilles de Laval
- **TITLES:** "Baron de Rais"
- **BIRTH:** Autumn, 1404
- **DEATH:** October 26, 1440

## WHO WAS HE?

He was a fifteenth-century French nobleman, soldier, and occultist who tortured, raped, and murdered scores of young children.

## EARLY INFLUENCES

He was born into one of the wealthiest families in France. He was raised by a nurse and rarely saw his parents and when they died around 1415 he was placed under the tutelage of his godfather, Jean de Craon. He was trained in the classic and military arts and humanities, and was a bright student. He was married off to wealthy heiress Catherine de Thouars of Brittany and spent several years as a commander in the Royal Army, fighting alongside Joan of Arc. After he retired from military service he pursued a profligate lifestyle and became involved in the occult.

## WHAT DID HE DO THAT WAS SO WRONG?

He kidnapped, tortured, and murdered hundreds of peasant children. The murders were only discovered after he was investigated for kidnapping a clergyman named Jean le Ferron in May 1440. Forty-seven charges were brought against him, including "the conjuration of demons" and sexual perversion against children.

At his trial, Gilles claimed that he killed for the first time in the year his grandfather died, either 1432 or 1433. An accomplice in many of the crimes, Etienne Corrillaut, testified that many children were beheaded. After decapitation he and his accomplices would line up the heads and debate which child was the fairest.

## BODY COUNT

The number of murders is often estimated as between 80 and 200, but some historians believe the number to be as high as 800.

## FAMOUS QUOTES

"When the children were dead [I] kissed them and those who had the most handsome limbs and heads [I] held up to admire them.

# RICHARD RAMÍREZ

- **BIRTH NAME:** Richard Muñoz Ramírez
- **TITLES:** "Walk-in Killer," "Valley Intruder," "Night Stalker"
- **BIRTH:** February 29, 1960, El Paso, Texas, USA
- **DEATH:** still alive

## WHO IS HE?

He is a rapist and serial killer who operated in California between June 1984 and August 1985.

## EARLY INFLUENCES

Quite apart from growing up with a violent father, Ramírez experienced several incidents during his childhood that must have desensitized and traumatized him. His cousin, a Vietnam veteran, enjoyed boasting about how he raped and killed Vietnamese women, and had the Polaroid photos to prove it. Ramírez also witnessed this same cousin murder his wife.

## WHAT DID HE DO THAT WAS SO WRONG?

His first victim, a seventy-nine-year-old woman, was murdered on the warm evening of June 28, 1984, at Glassel Park, Los Angeles. He climbed in a window she had left open to cool down her apartment, then raped and beat her before stabbing and nearly decapitating her.

Ramírez didn't kill again until March 1985, when he embarked on a ten-week frenzy of rape and murder. He shot a twenty-two-year-old woman outside her condo, but the bullet bounced off the keys in her hand, and she survived, but Ramírez shot her roommate dead. An hour later he pulled a thirty-year old woman out of her car and shot her several times. Three days later he abducted an eight-year-old girl, sexually assaulted and murdered her. His next victims were a married couple; he mutilated the wife's body. The corpses were discovered by their son.

Two months later he attacked another married couple: Harold Wu, aged sixty-six was shot dead, and his wife was beaten and violently raped, but not killed. At the end of May he attacked two women in their eighties with a hammer, one of whom survived. The next day he raped and sodomised a middle-aged mother while her twelve-year-old son was locked in the closet. During the next two months

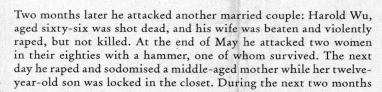

he killed three more people, raped a six-year-old girl and a sixty-three-year-old woman, and beat a sixteen-year-old girl almost to death with a tire iron. He attacked another married couple, and after killing the husband he molested the wife, and sodomized their son. After several more rapes and murders he broke into the home of a couple in their twenties. He shot the man and raped the woman, and tied her up, but she saw him drive off in an orange Toyota station wagon. Soon the police were able to identify Ramírez and broadcast his mug shot on national television. The next day he was almost beaten to death by an angry mob after being recognized as the "Night Stalker" while attempting to steal a car.

## BODY COUNT

Ramírez was found guilty of 13 counts of murder, 5 attempted murders, 11 sexual assaults, and 14 burglaries. His victims ranged in age from six to seventy-nine.

## FAMOUS QUOTES

"I love to kill people."

"You maggots make me sick . . . You don't understand me. You are not expected to. You are not capable of it. I am beyond your experience. I am beyond good and evil . . . Lucifer dwells within us all. That's it." (Excerpt of Richard Ramírez's statement before he received sentencing at his trial)

# JOEL RIFKIN

- **BIRTH NAME:** Evan Glaser
- **TITLES:** "The Turtle," "Joel the Ripper"
- **BIRTH:** January 20, 1959, New York, USA
- **DEATH:** still alive

## WHO IS HE?

He is New York's most prolific serial killer, operating between 1989 and 1993.

## EARLY INFLUENCES

At birth he was put up for adoption by his unwed college student parents, and he grew up in East Meadow, a suburban town on Long Island, New York. He was a shy and awkward child, who was incessantly bullied at school and was unsuccessful with girls. He was a poor student: despite a measured IQ of 128 he had undiagnosed dyslexia. After school he went to several different community colleges and dropped out of all of them. He lived at home, did several odd jobs, and hired prostitutes with what little spare cash he cold scrape together.

When Rifkin was twenty-eight his father, already dying from cancer, committed suicide and he became increasingly depressed and withdrawn. In August of the same year he was arrested for soliciting sex from an undercover policewoman, but he didn't tell his mother. He committed his first murder two years later.

## WHAT DID HE DO THAT WAS SO WRONG?

His first victim was a prostitute and drug addict. Rifkin beat her to death with a twelve-pound souvenir howitzer shell and then strangled her. He dismembered her body in the basement. He stuffed her head into a paint can and the other body parts into separate trash bags, then he scattered the remains in the woods and the East River.

Over the next four years he killed another sixteen women, mainly drug addicts and prostitutes. He killed some of them in his car, and others he invited back to his mother's house when he knew she would be away for a few days. He dismembered the bodies with a chain saw and dumped them around upstate New York and along the Harlem and Hudson Rivers.

He was finally caught when police picked him up for having no license plates on his Mazda pickup truck. After a high-speed chase Rifkin crashed into a telephone pole and police discovered the body of his final victim, twenty-two-year-old Tiffany Bresciani under a tarp in the back of the truck. He had killed her several days earlier and had a thick layer of Noxema smeared across his mustache to help counteract the stench of decay.

Rifkin was found guilty of nine murders in 1994 and sentenced to 203 years to life. He will be eligible for parole in 2197.

## BODY COUNT
He killed seventeen women during a four-year period.

## FAMOUS QUOTES
"There were nights I'd be with more than one girl. One girl would walk away fine, the other would end up dead."

"She was a prostitute. I picked her up on Allen Street in Manhattan. I had sex with her, then things went bad and I strangled her. Do you think I need a lawyer?"

# MARQUIS DE SADE

- **BIRTH NAME:** Donatien Alphonse François
- **TITLES:** "Marquis de Sade"
- **BIRTH:** June 2, 1740, Paris, France
- **DEATH:** December 2, 1814, natural causes, in his sleep

## WHO WAS HE?

He was a French aristocrat and writer of violent, sexually explicit works. His name has become synonymous with "Sadism."

## EARLY INFLUENCES

He was born in the Condé palace in Paris; his father was a compte and his mother was a lady-in-waiting of the princess of Condé. He attended a Jesuit school and then joined the army. He fought in the Seven Years War and then left the army to enter into an arranged marriage with the daughter of a rich magistrate.

## WHAT DID HE DO THAT WAS SO WRONG?

Shortly after his marriage he adopted an immoral libertine lifestyle.
He regularly abused young prostitutes and his own employees in his
castle in Lacoste. He kidnapped and abused scores of children and
young women and sexually mistreated hundreds of others, including members of his own family. Later his wife joined in. He had been
exiled to his castle after the authorities received complaints from
several prostitutes about being abused by him.

In 1772 he was sentenced to death for the non-lethal poisoning of
four prostitutes with an aphrodisiac, and for sodomizing his male
servant. He and his wife fled to Italy, where de Sade had an affair
with her sister. After a short imprisonment, he returned to Lacoste
and continued his debauchery.

He appealed against his death sentence in 1778, but his mother-in-
law had him imprisoned first at Vincennes and later the Bastille,
where he caused a near riot by shouting, "They are killing the prisoners here" and obscenities to the crowd outside. Two days later he
was sent to an insane asylum near Paris.

He wrote obscene works, including his epic *The 120 Days of Sodom*. His
violent and misogynistic books describe every torture imaginable.

## BODY COUNT

It isn't known how many women he killed (if any), but he was responsible for scores of rapes, and tortures, and he was the exemplary
woman-hating pornographer of all time.

## FAMOUS QUOTES

"Sex without pain is like food without taste."

"Here am I: at one stroke incestuous, adulteress, sodomite, and all that
in a girl who only lost her maidenhead today! What progress, my friends
. . . with what rapidity I advance along the thorny road of vice!"

"Your body is the church where Nature asks to be reverenced."

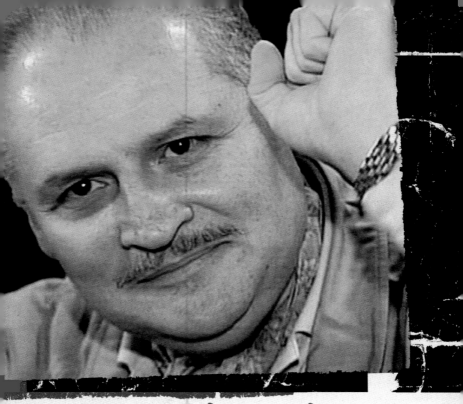

# ILICH RAMÍREZ SÁNCHEZ

- **BIRTH NAME:** Ilich Ramírez Sánchez
- **TITLES:** "Carlos the Jackal"
- **BIRTH:** October 12, 1949, Caracas, Venezuela
- **DEATH:** still alive

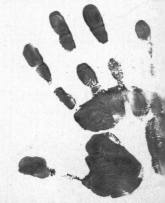

## WHO IS HE?

He is a Venezuelan-born terrorist and mercenary who operated between the early 1970s until his arrest in 1994.

## EARLY INFLUENCES

His father was a Marxist lawyer who christened him "Ilich" after Lenin, and he joined the national Communist youth movement when he was ten. He speaks five languages. In his teens he attended a guerrilla warfare summer camp run by the Cuban state intelligence agency, and then he continued his studies in London and a university in Moscow, from which he was expelled. Then he attended another guerrilla training camp run by the Popular Front for the Liberation of Palestine (PFLP).

## WHAT DID HE DO THAT WAS SO WRONG?

He performed his first act of terrorism in 1973 for the PFLP, when he attempted to assassinate the vice-president of the British Zionist Federation. He was responsible for a failed bomb attack on the Bank Hapoalim in London, car bomb attacks on three French newspapers, and killed two people and injured thirty with a grenade attack at a Parisian restaurant.

He was captured in 1975, but he escaped after shooting two detectives. This was followed by two bazooka attacks on El Al aircraft at Orly Airport in Paris, in January 1975. He then led the six-person team which attacked an OPEC meeting taking sixty hostages.

After settling in Aden he set up his own group, the Organization of Arab Armed Struggle, which trained terrorists in guerrilla warfare techniques for a number of years and formed links with the East German Stasi, Iraq's Saddam Hussein, and Cuba's Fidel Castro. He also assassinated Romanian dissidents for the Romanian Securitate. He masterminded a failed attack on a nuclear power station and several bombings in France and Germany. He recently voiced his support for Osama Bin Laden's attacks on the United States.

## BODY COUNT

He killed two people and injured thirty with a grenade attack at a Parisian restaurant, and multiple casualties were caused by the OPEC hostage crisis. Nine passengers were killed, and dozens more injured during three bomb attacks on French trains in March 1982 and December 1983.

## FAMOUS QUOTES

"I live out of a suitcase, I never get enough sleep and I don't see my family and friends as often as I would like. But I consider myself very fortunate."

"The way you say it, it sounds bad. It's not true that I just put on a few clothes and get a check for it afterwards."

# JOSEPH MOBUTU-SESE SEKO

**BIRTH NAME:** Joseph-Désiré Mobutu

**TITLES:** "Mobutu Sese Seko Kuku Ngbendu Wa Za Banga" (The all-powerful warrior who, because of his endurance and inflexible will to win, will go from conquest to conquest, leaving fire in his wake), "President of the Republic," "Father of the Nation," "Savior of the People," "Supreme Combatant"

**BIRTH:** October 14, 1930, Lisala, Belgian Congo

**DEATH:** September 7, 1997, prostate cancer

## WHO WAS HE?

He was the President of the Republic of Zaire (now the Democratic Republic of Congo) for thirty-two years (1965–1997).

## EARLY INFLUENCES

He was born into the Ngbandi ethnic group. His father died when he was young, and he was raised by his mother. He went to school in Léopoldville, and later in a Catholic mission boarding school.

He started his climb to power as a lowly soldier in the Belgian Congolese army, the Force Publique, rising to the rank of sergeant major. He left the army to become a journalist, then after independence in 1960 he became chief of staff of the army. A few months later Mobutu and President Joseph Kasavubu overthrew the Prime Minister Patrice Lumumba in a coup d'état (with the support of CIA agents and Belgian mercenaries). Five years later Mobutu overthrew Kasavubu.

## WHAT DID HE DO THAT WAS SO WRONG?

As soon as he came to power he consolidated his position by immediately suspending all political party activity (on the grounds that politicians had ruined the country). He declared a state of emergency then set about publicly executing hundreds of political rivals before large audiences and created a personality cult. Africans were made to abandon their Christian names in favor of African ones and all western clothing was banned—to be replaced by one-piece tunic called an abacost.

Although his regime temporarily suppressed tribal conflicts and was relatively stable and peaceful, his economic mismanagement and kleptocracy ruined the country. He personally siphoned off an estimated 4 billion dollars (mostly into Swiss bank accounts) while his people starved. He built several palaces, each costing millions of dollars (his first palace reportedly cost over $500 million).

Systematic torture was widespread, until Mobutu switched tactics and concentrated on bribing his opponents. In 1997, Mobutu was overthrown, and retired to the Cote d'Azur.

## BODY COUNT

Mobutu's regime tortured and killed thousands of political opponents. One example was the fate of Pierre Mulele, the former Minister of Education under Lumumba. In 1968 he returned from exile expecting a pardon. Instead his eyes were gouged out, his genitals removed, and his limbs amputated while he was still alive.

## FAMOUS QUOTES

"I have a clear conscience. I am an honest man. I have not pocketed one dollar of the people's money."

"It is better to die of hunger than to be rich and a slave to colonialism."

"In a word, everything is for sale; anything can be bought in our country."

# SUSAN SMITH

- **BIRTH NAME:** Susan Leigh Vaughan
- **TITLES:** "Baby Killer"
- **BIRTH:** September 26, 1971, Union, South Carolina, USA
- **DEATH:** still alive

## WHO IS SHE?

As a young mother she murdered her two pre-school children in 1994 by pushing her car into a lake with them inside.

## EARLY INFLUENCES

Her mother was a homemaker and her father was a fire fighter. Her childhood was blighted by her parents' volatile marriage, during which her alcoholic father was violent and made death threats. Before Susan entered preschool her half-brother attempted suicide by hanging himself. She was an unhappy and distant child, but she idolized her father. When Susan was six years old her parents divorced and her father committed suicide. Two weeks later her mother married a man whom Susan later claimed sexually molested her when she was in her teens. She did well at school and during her senior year of high school was voted "Friendliest Female." By this time her apparent outgoing nature hid deep insecurity and a desperate need for male attention. She attempted suicide twice by taking an overdose of aspirin, once when she was thirteen, and again four years later.

When she was seventeen she began dating an old high school friend, David Smith. He was already engaged to another girl, and considered his relationship with Susan to be casual. However they decided to get married when she became pregnant by him a year later.

The hasty marriage was doomed from the start. They both had extramarital affairs and separated several times during the next few years, but they remained devoted parents to their two young children. Weeks after their second child was born they decided to divorce and in January 1994 Susan began dating a rich and eligible bachelor, Tom Findlay. She had found being a single parent very difficult and finally she felt that her life was coming together. However, Tom was put off by her neediness and on October 17, 1994, he sent her a letter breaking off their relationship. One of the reasons he gave for the split was: "There are some things about you that aren't suited for me, and yes, I am speaking about your children."

## WHAT DID SHE DO THAT WAS SO WRONG?

In despair at being dumped, twenty-three-year-old Susan put her two children into her burgundy Mazda and drove along Highway 49 to John D. Long Lake. She drove to the end of a seventy-five-foot boat ramp and climbed out. Her pre-school sons were asleep in the back. She put the car in neutral and pushed it into the lake. She watched as it slowly slid underneath the water and sank to the bottom eighteen feet below.

Next she ran to a nearby house and claimed that a black man had stolen her car with her children inside. She stuck to this story for nine days, and the tragedy became national news, until worn down by hours of questioning about inconsistencies in her story, and after several polygraph tests in which she was shown to be lying when asked, "Do you know where your children are?" she confessed. Divers found the car upside down at the bottom of the lake and filled with water; the dead children were still strapped into their car seats.

She was given a sentence of thirty years to life, and will be eligible for parole in 2025.

## BODY COUNT

She killed her two young children, Michael, aged three and Alex, aged fourteen months.

## FAMOUS QUOTES

"Please help me! He's got my kids and he's got my car. A black man has got my kids and my car."

"No man would make me hurt my children. They were my life."

# HAROLD SHIPMAN

- **BIRTH NAME:** Harold Frederick Shipman
- **TITLES:** "Fred"
- **BIRTH:** January 14, 1946, Nottingham, UK
- **DEATH:** January 13, 2004, suicide (hanged)

## WHO WAS HE?

He was a British general practitioner who killed around 250 of his patients over three decades, in Hyde, Greater Manchester, beginning in the 1970s. He is the most prolific serial killer in the history of Britain.

## EARLY INFLUENCES

He was born in Nottingham and was the second of three children. His mother died from lung cancer when he was seventeen. He gained his medical degree at Leeds University where he met his future wife, Primrose. They married in 1966 and went on to have four children. He became a GP in Todmorden, in 1974. The following year he was caught forging prescriptions of pethidine (an opioid painkiller) for his own use, and spent a brief time in a drug rehabilitation clinic. It was around this time that he began murdering his patients.

## WHAT DID HE DO THAT WAS SO WRONG?

In March 1998, Dr. Linda Reynolds, from the Brooker Surgery in Hyde, across the road from Shipman's clinic, reported to the police her suspicions that he was killing his patients, due to the high number of cremation forms for elderly women that he had asked her to countersign.

A police investigation began, but inexperienced officers were placed on the case and they failed to make an arrest. The case was dropped, and Shipman was only reinvestigated because he forged the will of his last victim, Kathleen Grundy, disinheriting her daughter and giving £386,000 to himself. Grundy's body was exhumed and traces of diamorphine were found in her body. The police investigated the deaths of all his others patients of which fifteen were picked as test cases. Shipman was found guilty and sentenced to life imprisonment.

Most of Shipman's victims were elderly ladies in good health. He often killed them during a home visit, and then forged their medical records to make it seem that they had been very ill.

Shipman hanged himself using bed sheets attached to the bars of his cell, so that his wife could receive a National Health Service widow's pension.

## BODY COUNT

Four hundred and fifty-nine patients died under Shipman's care, of which at least 260 are thought to have been murdered. He is believed to have killed fifteen of his victims, including a four-year-old girl, while he was training as a junior doctor.

## FAMOUS QUOTES

"I feel responsible for the deaths of fifty-eight of my patients."

# RICHARD FRANKLIN SPECK

- ► **BIRTH NAME:** Richard Franklin Speck
- ► **TITLES:** "Nurse Killer"
- ► **BIRTH:** December 6, 1941, Kirkwood, Illinois, USA
- ► **DEATH:** December 5, 1991, heart attack

## WHO WAS HE?

He was a spree killer and rapist who murdered eight student nurses on one night in July 1966.

## EARLY INFLUENCES

Born in Illinois, the seventh of eight children, Speck moved to Dallas, Texas after the death of his father. His alcoholic stepfather frequently beat him and he sustained a head injury by falling from a tree. He was a poor student, who was always in trouble with the authorities. When he was twenty he married fifteen-year-old Shirley Malone, whom he frequently battered and raped.

## WHAT DID HE DO THAT WAS SO WRONG?

By the time he was twenty-five he had been arrested thirty-seven times for drunkenness, disorderly conduct, and burglary. It was unknown at the time that he had also raped sixty-five-year-old Virgil Harris, and beat to death Mary Kay Pierce, a barmaid who had rejected his advances. Six months before he killed the student nurses, his wife filed for divorce.

Late in the evening of July 13, 1966, Speck climbed through a window of a nurses' residence at South Chicago Community Hospital. He was high on a mixture of alcohol, the barbiturate Seconal, and a drug which he had acquired from a group of sailors and injected. He knocked on the door of one of the dorms where six student nurses were in bed. Speck threatened them with a gun, saying he wasn't going to hurt them, that he needed their money. He tied them up with strips of bed sheets, and when three more girls arrived, he tied them up as well. Then he killed them one by one, taking girls one at a time into another room, and stabbing and strangling them.

When the killing started some girls hid under the beds, but Speck pulled them all out, except for Corazon Amurao, who remained undetected. He raped and sodomized his eighth and final victim because she looked like his wife. After strangling her he left, and Amurao remained in her hiding place until 5:00 P.M. the following afternoon before raising the alarm. Police took her to hospital where she was able to give a very good photo fit description of the killer. Two days later Speck was arrested after a failed suicide attempt. He was sentenced to 1,200 years in prison, where he died ninteen years later.

## BODY COUNT

Speck killed eight student nurses, and barmaid Mary Kay Pierce, and it is likely that he committed several rapes. He was probably involved in the disappearance of three girls from Dunes Park in July of 1966.

## FAMOUS QUOTES

"I'm not going to hurt you. I'm only going to tie you up. I need your money to go to New Orleans."

"Born to Raise Hell." (Tattoo on his left forearm)

# JOSEPH STALIN

- **BIRTH NAME:** Iosif Vissarionovich Dzhugashvili
- **TITLES:** "Koba," "General Secretary of the Central Committee of the Communist Party of the Soviet Union"
- **BIRTH:** December 18, 1878, Gori, Georgia
- **DEATH:** March 5, 1953, brain hemorrhage

## WHO WAS HE?

He was the leader of the Soviet Union from 1924 to his death in 1953.

## EARLY INFLUENCES

His father was a violent alcoholic who often beat him and his mother. He died when he was eleven but a school friend wrote, "Those undeserved and fearful beatings made the boy as hard and heartless as his father." His doting mother wanted him to become a priest, and he attended a Jesuit seminary, but quit to spend a decade working in the revolutionary underground. In 1913 he adopted the name "Stalin" which means "man of steel." He became General Secretary of the Soviet Communist Party in 1922 and took over control of the country after Lenin's death in 1924 and began to violently crush all opposition.

## WHAT DID HE DO THAT WAS SO WRONG?

He was one of the most murderous dictators in human history. He ruthlessly purged all opposition to his regime, including the Red Army, which severely weakened his ability to fight Hitler. The 1930s witnessed the greatest purging activity to expel "opportunists" and "counter-revolutionary infiltrators." During the Great Terror, millions disappeared or were sent to forced labor camps in Siberia and Central Asia. After using the Communist Secret Police to murder hundreds of thousands of people, he purged the organization to cover his tracks.

As soon as he came to power he collectivized farming by abolishing private ownership and combining small farms into large-scale units. This was supposed to increase agricultural production by 50 percent, but instead it caused widespread famine as well as the execution of the hundreds of thousands of peasants who resisted. Despite this fall in production Stalin exported millions of tons of grain in exchange for money which never reached the people.

Stalin was also sexually deviant. He had the KGB abduct scores of young girls for his sexual pleasure.

## BODY COUNT

His purges and deportations to punish "anti-Soviet activities," led to the deaths of sixty million people. It is estimated that twenty-five million people died as a result of collectivization.

## FAMOUS QUOTES

"Ideas are more powerful than guns. We would not let our enemies have guns, why should we let them have ideas."

"A single death is a tragedy, a million deaths is a statistic."

# CHARLES STARKWEATHER

- **BIRTH NAME:** Charles Starkweather
- **TITLES:** "Spree Killer"
- **BIRTH:** November 24, 1938, Lincoln, Nebraska, USA
- **DEATH:** June 25, 1959, electric chair (executed)

## WHO WAS HE?

He was a spree killer who murdered eleven victims in Nebraska and Wyoming during a road trip with his underage girlfriend, Caril Ann Fugate. His actions inspired several movies, including *Natural Born Killers*, *Badlands*, and *Wild at Heart*.

## EARLY INFLUENCES

Charles Starkweather appears to have enjoyed a stable and comfortable home life. He was the third of seven children, and despite being born into a poor family during the Great Depression he claimed that he never went hungry. His school life was very different: he was bullied because of a mild speech impediment, bowed legs, and severe nearsightedness. He reacted to this treatment by becoming a bully himself, and as his physical confidence and self-loathing grew, he changed from a well-behaved child into one of the meanest, toughest kids in the neighborhood. He also became obsessed with James Dean and tried to imitate his mannerisms, clothes, and hairstyle.

He quit school at sixteen and started working in a warehouse. A few years later he started dating thirteen-year-old Caril Ann Fugate. After his father kicked him out of the house for crashing his car, he became a garbage man (he was later sacked). Believing he was doomed to a lifetime of drudgery and poverty, he started plotting bank robberies and developed his guiding belief that "dead people are all on the same level."

## WHAT DID HE DO THAT WAS SO WRONG?

His first murder took place on November 30, 1957. He had tried to buy a stuffed toy for his girlfriend from a gas station, but had been refused credit. He returned at three in the morning with a 12-gauge shotgun, robbed $100 from the till and, after a scuffle, he shot the attendant in the head at point blank range. After the killing he felt invincible, that he had risen above the laws of man and could do as he pleased. Two months later following an argument with Caril Ann's mother and stepfather at their house, he shot them and stabbed Caril Ann's two-year-old sister. After staying in the house for a week, with a sign on the front door saying everyone inside had flu, the couple went on the road and shot and stabbed a further seven people. After a manhunt involving over a thousand police officers, they were arrested in Douglas, Wyoming.

## BODY COUNT

Starkweather murdered eleven victims, and Caril Ann Fugate's role in the killings was never determined.

## FAMOUS QUOTES

"Dead people are all on the same level."

"The more I looked at people, the more I hated them because I knowed there wasn't any place for me with the kind of people I knowed . . . A bunch of Goddamned sons of bitches looking for somebody to make fun of . . . some poor fellow who ain't done nothin' but feed chickens."

# HAJI MOHAMMAD SUHARTO

- **BIRTH NAME:** Haji Mohammad Soeharto
- **TITLES:** "President of Indonesia"
- **BIRTH:** June 8, 1921, Kemusuk, Indonesia
- **DEATH:** still alive

## WHO IS HE?

He is the former Indonesian military and political leader, President of Indonesia from 1967 to 1998.

## EARLY INFLUENCES

He was born into a peasant ethnic-Javanese family, and grew up without electricity or running water. Details of his early life are unclear, but widely thought to have been unstable. His parents divorced while he was very young and he was estranged from both parents at various times. Since he received a reasonable education, inconsistent with being a peasant, it is plausible that he was the illegitimate child of a well-off benefactor.

After a brief period working in a bank, he joined the Dutch military in 1940. When the Dutch surrendered to the Japanese, Suharto switched allegiance and joined the occupying police force as a keibuho (assistant inspector), where he acquired intelligence training that was vital to his later regime. After Japanese surrender he joined the Indonesian army and distinguished himself fighting against the Dutch for independence.

In 1955 the first democratic elections took place, the Indonesian National Union Party took control, and Suharto rose through the military until by 1965 he was commander of the army.

## WHAT DID HE DO THAT WAS SO WRONG?

In March 1966 Suharto gained supreme power of the country and ruled for the next three decades with a staunch anti-Communist agenda. After suppressing an attempted coup from the Indonesian Communist Party (PKI), all leftist organizations and trade unions were banned and Suharto led a purge against PKI members and Chinese, and more than million people were murdered in what became one of the most massive and violent political purges of the twentieth century.

Fearing that East Timor was becoming a Communist threat, Indonesia invaded the country in December 1975 and installed a puppet government. This was followed by the systematic killing of anyone suspected of having Communist sympathies.

## BODY COUNT

His regime was responsible for the murder of more than a million people following the coup attempt in 1965.

It is estimated that 60,000 East Timorese or 10 percent of the population were killed during the first two months of the invasion. A total of 250,000 East Timorese have died during the occupation (nearly 40 percent of the 1975 population).

## FAMOUS QUOTES

"You know, what you regard as corruption in your part of the world, we regard as family values."

"If I am no longer trusted, I will become a pandito [sage] and endeavor to get closer to God."

# KIM IL-SUNG

- **BIRTH NAME:** Kim Sung-ju
- **TITLES:** "Great Leader," "Eternal President"
- **BIRTH:** April 15, 1912, Nam-ri, South P'yŏngan Province, Korea
- **DEATH:** July 8, 1994, heart attack

## WHO WAS HE?

He was the leader of North Korea from its founding in 1948 until his death.

## EARLY INFLUENCES

When he was born, Korea was under Japanese occupation. He grew up and went to school in north-eastern China where he became interested in Communism and was arrested for joining a subversive student group. He was a member of several anti-Japanese guerrilla groups including the Chinese-led Northeast Anti-Japanese United Army of which he became a commander in 1941. After the Japanese drove the guerrillas from northern China, Kim fled to Russia and served a brief spell with the Soviet Red Army. After the Second World War he returned to Korea, became head of the Provisional People's Committee, and began to consolidate his power with the first of many purges.

## WHAT DID HE DO THAT WAS SO WRONG?

For half a century he ruled by assassinating opposition and imprisoning and torturing dissidents. He established a work camp system and imprisoned for life over 200,000 "political" prisoners for crimes against the state, including such trivial misdemeanors as reading a foreign newspaper, or singing a South Korean pop song.

He developed a messianic personality cult and everyone in the country had to call him "Great Leader." A birth myth described how he was born in a log cabin on North Korea's most scared mountain under a bright star and a double rainbow.

The Soviets supplied military advisors and extensive weaponry, and then in June 1950 Kim started the Korean War by attacking South Korea in order to reunify the country, which had been partitioned five years earlier. After several years of fighting Kim attempted to reconstruct the country by cutting off trade links and followed a policy of Juche, or austere self-sufficiency. He established a Soviet-style command economy with a huge industrial armament program and agricultural collectivism. Kim spent most of his country's wealth on armaments, while his people starved. North Korea became more and more impoverished and backward, while capitalist South Korea thrived. Kim also established "Pleasure Brigades" from groups of school girls for his sexual gratification and that of high party members.

## BODY COUNT

About three million people were killed in the Korean War and between 600,000 and one million North Koreans starved to death because of his economic policies.

## FAMOUS QUOTES

"Factionalists or enemies of class, whoever they are, their seed must be eliminated through three generations."

"The great leader Comrade Kim Il-Sung looked upon his people as his God, loved them dearly, trusted them deeply and devoted everything to the cause of their freedom and happiness while he himself suffered hardships of every description throughout his life."

# PETER SUTCLIFFE

- **BIRTH NAME:** Peter William Sutcliffe
- **TITLES:** "Yorkshire Ripper"
- **BIRTH:** June 2, 1946, Bingley, West Yorkshire, UK
- **DEATH:** still alive

## WHO IS HE?

He is a serial killer who was convicted of the murders of thirteen women in the north of England and attacks on seven more between 1975 and 1980.

## EARLY INFLUENCES

He was the son of a mill worker, but as a quiet sensitive child who idolized his mother, he was a disappointment to his masculine father. He was bullied at school which he left at fifteen and did various low-paid jobs, including working as a grave digger. He met Sonia Szurma in 1966 and they married eight years later. After receiving a redundancy payment from a factory, he gained an HGV license and became a truck driver. Sonia took a teacher training course, and suffered several miscarriages, after which they were told they could not have children.

## WHAT DID HE DO THAT WAS SO WRONG?

He committed his first attack in July 4, 1975. Thirty-six-year-old Anna Rogulskyj was walking home alone in Keighley, Yorkshire, when Sutcliffe attacked her from behind with a ball-peen hammer, then he slashed her stomach with a knife. He fled after being disturbed and she survived after a twelve-hour operation during which she was given the last rites.

His modus operandi was to hit women with his ball-peen hammer then stab them repeatedly.

During the hunt for the "Yorkshire Ripper," police conducted 250,000 interviews and made 21,000 house searches. Sutcliffe was interviewed a staggering eleven times and never charged. The police investigation was thrown off track for several months by a hoax taped message by a man with a Wearside accent, and the hunt for the Ripper switched from Yorkshire to the North East. (The hoaxer,

John Samuel Humble, was finally tracked down on October 20, 2005, and was sentenced to eight years in jail for perverting the course of justice.)

Sutcliffe was eventually arrested for drunk driving. Before getting into the police car he asked permission to urinate. He went behind the bushes and dumped his weapons, which were only discovered the next day when the arresting officer returned to the spot on a hunch and recovered a knife, hammer, and rope. After two days of questioning, on the afternoon of January 4, 1981, Sutcliffe calmly confessed.

## BODY COUNT

He attacked at least twenty women aged between sixteen and forty-seven, killing thirteen of them and leaving seven others emotionally and physically scarred.

## FAMOUS QUOTES

"Killing prostitutes had become an obsession with me. I could not stop myself. It was like a drug."

"The women I killed were filth—bastard prostitutes who were littering the streets. I was just cleaning up the place a bit."

# HIDEKI TOJO

- **BIRTH NAME:** Hideki Tojo
- **TITLES:** "The Razor," "Prime Minister"
- **BIRTH:** December 30, 1884, Tokyo, Japan
- **DEATH:** December 23, 1948, hanged (executed)

## WHO WAS HE?

He was a general in the Imperial Japanese Army and the fortieth Prime Minister of Japan.

## EARLY INFLUENCES

He was the third son of a Lieutenant General in the Japanese Army. Both his brothers died before he was born. A fanatical nationalist, he graduated from military academy in 1905 and worked his way up through the ranks until by May 1940 he was appointed minister for war and he became prime minister of Japan the following year. He also led the Japanese Secret Service before and during the Pacific War.

## WHAT DID HE DO THAT WAS SO WRONG?

A supporter and admirer of the nationalism of Nazi Germany, as head of the military he pushed Japan into the Second World War and ordered the attack on Pearl Harbor on December 7, 1941, despite the fact that Emperor Hirohito preferred to follow the path of negotiation.

After realizing that he couldn't win the war, he attempted suicide by shooting himself in the chest just before his arrest by the US military in 1945. He was nursed back to health and tried for war crimes and found guilty of count 1 (waging wars of aggression, and war or wars in violation of international law), count 27 (waging unprovoked war against China), count 29 (waging aggressive war against the United States), count 31 (waging aggressive war against the British Commonwealth), count 32 (waging aggressive war against the Netherlands), count 33 (waging aggressive war against France (Indochina)), and count 54 (ordering, authorizing, and permitting inhumane treatment of Prisoners of War [POWs] and others).

## BODY COUNT

Tojo's regime was responsible for the murder of more than eight million civilians in China, Korea, Philippines, Indochina, and other Pacific islands. Tens of thousands of Allied POWs were executed and biological experiments were performed on both POWs and Chinese civilians.

## FAMOUS QUOTES

"It is natural that I should bear entire responsibility for the war in general, and, needless to say, I am prepared to do so."

"Japan was ensuring the stability of East Asia while contributing to world peace."

"The moment the first American soldier sets foot on the Japanese mainland, all prisoners of war will be shot."

# JANE TOPPAN

- **BIRTH NAME:** Honora Kelly
- **TITLES:** "The Female Jack the Ripper"
- **BIRTH:** 1854, Boston, Massachusetts, USA
- **DEATH:** 1938, natural causes

## WHO WAS SHE?

She was an American nurse and serial killer who killed her patients with lethal doses of prescription medicines.

## EARLY INFLUENCES

She grew up in Lowell, Massachusetts, in a poor family, with a history of mental illness. When she was nine she went into an orphanage, after her mother died and her father was committed to a mental asylum for trying to sew his eyelids together. From here she was fostered by Ann Toppan, whom, Jane later claimed, treated her badly, while pouring affection on her own children. She became engaged, but after her fiancé dumped her for another woman, she became depressed and attempted suicide twice.

## WHAT DID SHE DO THAT WAS SO WRONG?

She admitted to getting a thrill from killing people. In 1885 Toppan trained as a nurse at Cambridge Hospital. She experimented on patients by giving them morphine and atrophine, and it is thought she killed at least twelve patients there. In 1889 she received good enough references to be given a job at the prestigious Massachusetts General Hospital, where she killed a few more patients and her foster sister Elizabeth with strychnine, before being fired a year later. She returned to Cambridge and became a private nurse. In 1901 she became the live-in carer of an old man called Alden Davis and his family, after he became a widower (Toppan had killed his wife). A few weeks later she killed Davis and two of his daughters. Then she poisoned her dead foster sister's husband and his sister. He survived and kicked her out of the house. Toppan was arrested in October 1901 after a postmortem on one of Davis's daughters suggested that she had been poisoned. She confessed to thirty-one murders and was sent to Taunton State Asylum for the Criminally Insane where she died thirty-six years later.

## BODY COUNT

She confessed to thirty-one murders but she is believed to have killed at least twice that number.

## FAMOUS QUOTES

"That is my ambition, to have killed more people—more helpless people—than any man or woman who has ever lived."

"I fooled them all—I fooled the stupid doctors and the ignorant relatives. I have been fooling them for years and years."

# TOMÁS DE TORQUEMADA

- **BIRTH NAME:** Tomás de Torquemada
- **TITLES:** "Grand Inquisitor of Spain"
- **BIRTH:** 1420, Torquemada, Spain
- **DEATH:** September 16, 1498

## WHO WAS HE?

He was a Dominican friar who set up the Spanish Inquisition, which tortured and killed thousands in the name of the Catholic Church during the Middle Ages.

## EARLY INFLUENCES

He was born into an illustrious Catholic family—his uncle was the eminent cardinal Juan de Torquemada. He entered a Dominican seminary in his youth, and later became Confessor to Princess Isabella. When she became queen in 1474 he became one of the most powerful men in Spain, but continued to live an austere life, sent his sister to a convent, gave away all his money, abstained from eating meat and always wore a hair shirt next to his skin.

## WHAT DID HE DO THAT WAS SO WRONG?

In 1483 he became Grand Inquisitor, and wrote the twenty-eight articles which formed the basis of his persecutions.

He developed an oppressive network of spies and secret police. Under his leadership the Spanish Inquisition scoured the country looking for heretics. Suspects were tortured for days on end until they confessed, by examiners who wore white gowns with black hoods. Tortures included stretching on a rack and being suspended by a rope from the ceiling and then dropped within inches of the floor— a painful early form of bungee jump with rope instead of elastic. Suspects could only be interrogated once, but this could last indefinitely, after which they were obliged to sign a confession. This just led to their being burned at the stake. Many of the victims begged to be told what they were accused of, so that they could confess.

Although Torquemada was of Jewish descent, he persuaded Ferdinand and Isabella to expel Jews from Spain, and persecuted Jews throughout his career, even those who had converted to Christianity.

Because he was so hated, he traveled with 50 mounted guards and 250 armed men.

## BODY COUNT

While he was Grand Inquisitor over two thousand heretics were burned at the stake and many more were tortured to death. After his death the Inquisition continued torturing and murdering for another two centuries.

## FAMOUS QUOTES

"[He was] the hammer of heretics, the light of Spain, the savior of his country, the honor of his order." (Sebastián de Olmedo, Spanish chronicler)

"There is only one crime I am guilty of . . . Being too merciful!"

# MARY TUDOR

- **BIRTH NAME:** Mary Tudor
- **TITLES:** "Mary I of England," "Bloody Mary"
- **BIRTH:** February 18, 1516, Greenwich, London, UK
- **DEATH:** November 17, 1558, ovarian cyst

## WHO WAS SHE?

She was the first Queen of England to rule in her own right, and she brutally persecuted the Protestants.

## EARLY INFLUENCES

She was the daughter of Henry VIII and Catherine of Aragon. She was a sickly child with poor eyesight and suffered from bad headaches. At the age of two she was engaged for the first time, to the Dauphin of France.

Mary received an excellent education and spoke Latin, French, Spanish, and understood Italian. She was declared illegitimate when Henry dissolved his marriage in 1533 so that he could marry Ann Boleyn. Mary was moved to Richmond and was not allowed to see her mother. She was no longer able to call herself a princess and she was made to renounce her Catholic faith, although she continued to worship in secret.

After her half-brother Edward VI died, Lady Jane Grey was placed on the throne by a Protestant uprising, and Mary fled to Norfolk. After less than two weeks on the throne, Jane Grey was executed and Mary became queen.

## WHAT DID SHE DO THAT WAS SO WRONG?

A soon as she had been crowned she tried to reintroduce Catholicism as the national religion, and she planned to marry the Catholic King of Spain, Philip. The Protestants, led by Sir Thomas Wyatt, rose up against her, but they were defeated and Mary executed the leaders of the "Wyatt Rebellion." After her marriage to Philip, which led England into a war with France, Mary began persecuting heretics. Her support of the papacy and the Roman Catholic Church meant that she unable to win the support of the nobles and most of her subjects, and she died after an unpopular five-year reign, to be replaced by her half-sister Elizabeth I.

## BODY COUNT

She had 283 heretics burned at the stake including the Archbishop of Canterbury, Thomas Cranmer, and killed the ringleaders of the Wyatt Rebellion.

## FAMOUS QUOTES

"Take me for your lawful daughter born in true matrimony. If I agreed to the contrary I should offend God; in all other things Your Highness shall find me an obedient daughter."

"While my father lives I shall be only the Lady Mary, the most unhappy lady in Christendom."

# MAO TSE-TUNG

- **BIRTH NAME:** Mao Tse-Tung
- **TITLES:** "Great Leader," "Chairman Mao"
- **BIRTH:** December 26, 1893, Shaoshan, Hunan province, China
- **DEATH:** September 9, 1976, Lou Gehrig's Disease

## WHO WAS HE?

He was the leader of China's Communist Revolution and ruled China from October 1, 1949, until his death.

## EARLY INFLUENCES

Despite claiming he was the son of a poor peasant, his father had worked his way up from poverty to become a wealthy farmer and grain merchant. Mao received a good education and later became the principal of a primary school, before becoming a revolutionary and politician. He began a series of peasant uprisings in 1927 and four years later became founder leader of the Chinese Soviet Republic in part of Kiangsi Province. Half his army was subsequently defeated and the survivors spent the next two years traveling 6,000 miles to the Soviet border, in what became known as the mythical "Long March." When the Japanese invaded, the Communists and Nationalists fought together, but after the Second World War, with huge Soviet backing, Mao defeated the Nationalists in a civil war and took overall power on October 1, 1949.

## WHAT DID HE DO THAT WAS SO WRONG?

During the first two years of power his regime executed three million political opponents. The landlord class was wiped out, but the peasants who had fought for control of the land soon found themselves starving in inefficient collectives as a result of Mao's first Five Year Plan, which introduced a massive program of industrialization.

Mao's next big failure was the "Hundred Flowers Campaign" in which he encouraged open criticism of the government: "Let a hundred flowers bloom, let all the schools of thought contend." His aim was to weaken his opponents in government, but when liberals and intellectuals began criticizing Mao, he quickly backtracked and announced that it was time to separate "fragrant flowers" from "poisonous weeds." Hundreds of thousands of dissenters and intellectuals were jailed and executed, or sent to work in the fields.

His third and most disastrous policy was the second Five Year Plan known as the "Great Leap Forward." This fast-track industrialization was intended to cram forty years of industrial expansion into five. Steel making was the priority and factories sprang up in villages across the country, with farming tools and domestic utensils being melted down to produce poor quality steel that the country did not need and could not use. The huge infrastructure projects such as dams and canals were also completely useless, as Mao had refused to consult qualified engineers.

As agricultural production plummeted and famine became widespread, corrupt and terrified local party officials covered up the figures and pretended that grain production was soaring year on year. Millions of people starved to death as a result of this policy.

Meanwhile Mao became one of the richest men in the country, with widespread publication of his *Little Red Book*. He lived in luxury, with numerous concubines and amassed the largest collection of pornography in the world.

## BODY COUNT

Between thirty and seventy million people died of famine because of Mao's disastrous policies, and many millions more were executed as enemies of the state.

## FAMOUS QUOTES

"Every Communist must grasp the truth: 'Political power grows out of the barrel of a gun.'"

"Communism is not love. Communism is a hammer which we use to crush the enemy."

"War can only be abolished through war, and in order to get rid of the gun it is necessary to take up the gun."

# IVAN IV VASILYEVICH

- **BIRTH NAME:** Ivan IV Vasilyevich
- **TITLES:** "Ivan the Terrible"
- **BIRTH:** August 25, 1530, Moscow, Russia
- **DEATH:** March 18, 1584, mercury poisoning

## WHO WAS HE?

He was the Grand Duke of Muscovy from 1533 to 1547 and was the first ruler of Russia to assume the title of tsar.

## EARLY INFLUENCES

Ivan had a traumatic and brutal childhood. His father died when he was three, his mother took power but was poisoned when Ivan was eight, and his beloved nurse was sent to a convent. The ruling boyars beat and sexually assaulted him, and Ivan was witness to many beatings and murders as two rival noble families fought each other in his castle. Powerless and brutalized, Ivan took out his own frustrations on defenseless animals—he tore the feathers off birds and threw dogs and cats from towers. When Ivan was thirteen he committed his first murder, he had Prince Andrew Shuisky locked in a cage with a pack of ravenous hunting dogs.

## WHAT DID HE DO THAT WAS SO WRONG?

Ivan brutally suppressed all opposition. He created a personal force of bodyguards called the Oprichniki ("The Ones Who Serve"). They wore black robes and rode black horses, carried a dog's head on a stick as their mascot, and rode around the country killing anyone Ivan disliked. Ivan and his bodyguards performed quasi-religious orgies in which scores of young men and women were raped and tortured. He also roamed the streets of Moscow raping and beating at will and had boyar wives sent into the woods to be hunted down like wild animals.

Other tortures included having peasant women strip naked for target practice; drowning scores of beggars in a lake; roasting traitors over a spit, frying them alive in giant cast iron skillets, or boiling them in oil. He murdered thousands of nobles and had the head of the Russian church killed when he begged for clemency for the people.

Ivan carried a stick with an iron tip, with which he beat anyone who caused him displeasure. He beat up his pregnant daughter-in-law because he disapproved of her clothing, so that she miscarried. After this he and his son got into a violent argument and Ivan hit him over the head. He fell into a coma and died of an infected wound a few days later.

He boasted of raping a thousand virgins, and had his seventh wife drowned when he discovered she was not a virgin.

Ivan was deeply religious and often paid local monasteries large sums of money to buy his salvation and salve his conscience. On his deathbed he took the religious vows of a monk.

## BODY COUNT

Hundreds of thousands of subjects died during his regime, and many more starved. Ivan's biggest atrocity was the slaughter of the inhabitants of an entire village of Novgorod in 1570. One person was killed every ten seconds, round the clock for seven days, with a death toll of over 60,000 men, women, and children. Babies were beaten to death while their parents watched.

## FAMOUS QUOTES

"Did I ascend the throne by robbery or armed bloodshed? I was born to rule by the grace of God; and I do not even remember my father bequeathing the throne to me."

"If you are so sure of your righteousness, why did you run away and not prefer martyrdom at my hands?"

# VLAD THE IMPALER

- **BIRTH NAME:** Vlad Dracula
- **TITLES:** "Vlad III," "Drakulya," (postmortem)
- **BIRTH:** 1431, Sighişoara, Transylvania
- **DEATH:** December 1476, mistakenly killed by his own men

## WHO WAS HE?

He was the fifteenth-century ruler of Wallachia, a Romanian principality in Eastern Europe. He was the inspiration for Bram Stoker's *Dracula*, written in 1897.

## EARLY INFLUENCES

His father, Vlad Dracul, was a knight of the Order of the Dragon, a secret fraternity founded by the Emperor in 1387 to defend Christianity. He took over the throne of Wallachia in 1436, but he subsequently betrayed the order by forming an alliance with the Turks, and the young Vlad and his brother were handed over to Sultan Murad II as an insurance policy to ensure he upheld the treaty. In 1447 Vlad's father was assassinated and he was set free. He returned home to discover his other brother, Mircea, had had his eyes gouged out and been buried alive by the boyars of Tirgoviste. At the age of twenty-five, Vlad reclaimed his throne by killing the orchestrator of the coup that had dethroned his father and had all the boyars arrested.

## WHAT DID HE DO THAT WAS SO WRONG?

Things went downhill as soon as he came to power. The captive boyars were either sent into slavery, building his Poenari Castle on the Arges River, or if they were old or infirm, they were publicly impaled.

Many slaves died while building his castle. Many worked naked because their clothes fell off with wear.

One day Vlad decided to end the suffering of the sick, poor and needy by inviting them to a lavish banquet in the great hall in Tirgoviste. After they were satiated, he told them that they would never have to suffer pain and hunger again. He then had his men board up the hall and burn it, roasting alive everyone inside.

On St. Bartholomew's Day he impaled 30,000 merchants for breaking trade laws, and left their rotting bodies outside the city as an example to others.

He is also rumored to have practiced cannibalism, and often decorated his banquets with impaled subjects and enemies. He practiced every imaginable form of torture, from skinning alive, to boiling, eviscerating and disfigurement. On one occasion when a group of Turkish ambassadors refused to remove their hats, he had them nailed to their heads.

Even when he was dethroned and imprisoned, he got his kicks from impaling rats and mice.

## FAMOUS QUOTES

"From the distinctly inadequate material at our disposal it is impossible to avoid the conclusion that Vlad was a man of diseased and abnormal tendencies, the victim of acute moral insanity." (R. W. Seton-Watson)

# FRED WEST & ROSEMARY WEST

- **BIRTH NAME:** Fred Walter Stephen West
- **TITLES:** "Serial Killer"
- **BIRTH:** September 29, 1941, Much Marcle, UK
- **DEATH:** January 1, 1995, suicide (hanged)

- **BIRTH NAME:** Rose Letts
- **TITLES:** "Serial Killer"
- **BIRTH:** November 29, 1953, Devon, UK
- **DEATH:** still alive

## WHO WERE THEY?

They were a married couple who raped, tortured, and murdered at least twelve young women between 1967 and 1994, including some of their own children and step-children.

## EARLY INFLUENCES

Fred West was the son of farm laborers. He was very close to his mother, but was lazy and unpromising at school, where he was bullied for being a "mamma's boy." He left school almost illiterate and became a farm hand. When he was seventeen he sustained serious head injuries in a motorcycle crash, and had a metal plate put in his head. Shortly after recovering he suffered another head trauma when he was pushed off a fire escape by a girl after sticking his hand up her skirt.

Rose was born to a schizophrenic abusive father and a severely depressive mother who was given electroconvulsive therapy while pregnant with her. She was of low intelligence and was overweight and unpopular at school, and had an aggressive temper. She was sexually precocious from her early teens, and fondled her younger brother sexually. He father forbade her from dating boys her own age, and Rose later alleged he had sexually abused her.

## WHAT DID THEY DO THAT WAS SO WRONG?

Fred committed his first major crime when he was twenty, raping a thirteen-year-old family friend and he was disowned by his family, but not jailed. He moved to Scotland where he accidentally ran over and killed a four-year-old boy with his ice-cream van. He married an ex-prostitute, Rena Costello, and she gave birth to Charmaine, who was not Fred's child. They moved back to Gloucester and Fred got a job in a slaughterhouse, which may have contributed to his developing a morbid obsession with dismemberment. Fred took a mistress, Anna McFall, and killed her in 1967 her when she became pregnant with his child. He cut her up and buried her in a field, keeping the fingers and kneecaps, a trophy pattern he repeated with every subsequent murder.

In late 1968 Fred met Rose Letts and she gave birth to Heather in October 1970. Some time in 1971 Rose lost her temper with Charmaine and murdered her. When Fred came out of prison (for failing to pay fines), he buried the body under the kitchen floor and used it as leverage against Rose for the rest of their relationship.

Fred and Rose both enjoyed brutal bondage sex, and he prostituted her to satisfy their sexual appetites (he watched through a peephole), and to make extra income. When Rena came looking for Charmaine, Fred killed her and buried her. In June 1972 they moved to Number 25, Cromwell Road in Gloucester, and Fred turned the cellar into his children's bedroom which doubled as a torture chamber, which they christened with Fred brutally raping his eight-year-old daughter Anne-Marie while Rose held her down. The basement became an ongoing home improvement project as more and more bodies were buried there over the next two decades.

In 1972 they took in a nanny, seventeen-year-old Caroline Owens, and raped her. They were found guilty in court, but incredibly, they both escaped with a fine, even though Fred had a criminal record and had threatened to kill and bury her. Over the following years several more young women were either abducted or enticed into their home as lodgers or to care for their children, including two fifteen-year-old schoolgirls. Their victims were raped, tortured, and sometimes kept as sex slaves for several days, before being murdered, dismembered, and buried under the cellar floor.

The Wests raped their own children, and their last known victim, killed in June 1987, was their sixteen-year-old daughter, Heather.

## BODY COUNT

It is believed that the Wests may have killed as many as thirty people but only twelve bodies have been found. Nine bodies were dug up from under 25 Cromwell Street, one was discovered beneath their previous home, and two more were found buried in fields near Much Marcle, Herefordshire.

There were at least eight sexual assaults committed in Gloucester that fit the pattern.

## FAMOUS QUOTES

"If attention is paid to what I think, you will never be released." (Mr. Justice Mantell to Rose West)

"I'll keep you in the cellar and let my black friends have you, and when we're finished we'll kill you and bury you under the paving stones of Gloucester." (Fred West's threat to rape victim Caroline Owens)

# CHRISTOPHER WILDER

- ▰ **BIRTH NAME:** Christopher Bernard Wilder
- ▰ **TITLES:** "The Beauty Queen Killer"
- ▰ **BIRTH:** March 13, 1945
- ▰ **DEATH:** April 13, 1984, shot

## WHO WAS HE?

He was one of America's most brutal and sadistic rapists and spree killers, who often targeted beauty queens, while posing as a fashion photographer.

## EARLY INFLUENCES

He was the oldest child of an American naval officer and an Australian woman. During his adolescence he was caught window-peeking, and at age seventeen he was arrested for taking part in the gang rape of a girl on a beach in Sydney, Australia. He pleaded guilty and received a year's probation and electroshock therapy.

At age twenty-three he married but his wife divorced him a few weeks later after finding naked pictures and women's panties in his briefcase. In 1969 he emigrated to the United States and settled in Florida, where his electrical and construction and real estate business made him relatively wealthy. In 1971 he was arrested for soliciting women to pose for nude photos, but he escaped with a small fine. In 1977 he went to court after forcing a high school student to have oral sex, but he was acquitted. In 1980, posing as a fashion photographer, he lured a woman to his truck where he drugged and raped her. He received five years probation and therapy. In 1982 he was in Australia visiting his parents when he was arrested for abducting two fifteen-year-old girls, tying them up, and molesting them. His parents posted bail and he fled back to Florida.

## WHAT DID HE DO THAT WAS SO WRONG?

He was obsessed with dominating women and turning them into sex slaves. In February 1984 he raped and killed two women, and then went on the run for three months during which time he raped and killed a further nine women, killing six of them.

He abducted a university student from a shopping mall in Tallahassee, drove her to a motel where he raped and tortured her. One of his victims in Beaumont, Texas, had told her husband two days prior to her disappearance that she had been approached by a man matching Wilder's description asking her to model for him. She had declined. Wilder snatched her two days later and killed her with multiple stab wounds. Four days later he killed again in Oklahoma City, and again at the end of March in Colorado, and Las Vegas, Nevada. He became one of the FBI's ten most wanted men. On April 2 he abducted a sixteen-year-old, raped her, and then kept her with him as he stabbed another two victims, one of whom survived. Then he spared her life and put her on a plane to Los Angeles. On April 13 he was shot during a struggle with state troopers at a gas station 10 miles from the Canadian border.

## BODY COUNT
He has been definitively linked to eight victims, but it is likely that he raped and murdered at least ten others between 1965 and 1984.

## FAMOUS QUOTES
"Through our investigation to date, through interviews of key people, we know Wilder has indicated if he were caught he would not be taken alive, and would kill himself." (James Greenleaf, FBI special agent)

# BO NE WIN

- **BIRTH NAME:** Shu Maung
- **TITLES:** "Big Father," "The Old Man," "Number One"
- **BIRTH:** July 10, 1910, Paungdale, Burma
- **DEATH:** December 5, 2002, natural causes

## WHO WAS HE?

He was a Burmese military commander and dictator of Burma from 1962 until 1988.

## EARLY INFLUENCES

He was born into an educated middle class family and was part Chinese. He spent two years at Rangoon University where he studied biology, then left early to join the anti-British nationalist group, Dobama Asiayone.

In 1941 he secretly traveled to Tokyo to receive military training from the Japanese and in 1943 became chief-of-staff of the pro-Japanese Burmese Independence Army (BIA). Following Burmese independence he became commander in chief of the armed forces. He then exploited ethnic conflicts to strengthen his own position.

## WHAT DID HE DO THAT WAS SO WRONG?

He won power in 1962 after a bloodless coup, and then attempted to create a Marxist one-party state which ruined the country's economy. He brutally suppressed all opposition and led repeated purges of the military. In the year he came to power dozens of students were shot dead during protests at Rangoon University, and the student union building was dynamited.

Ne Win cut off the country from the outside world and pursued the "Burmese Way to Socialism." Foreign businesses were forced to leave the country and all foreign investment ceased. By 1987 Ne Win's disastrous policies led the United Nations (UN) to designate the once prosperous country a "Least Developed Nation," one of the ten poorest nations in the world.

In 1988 student-led protests against the regime broke out in Rangoon, after Ne Win, who was obsessed with numerology, reissued bank notes in denominations divisible by the "auspicious" number nine, wiping out the savings of thousands of people overnight. This uprising became known as the "Rangoon Spring," and in August it spread across the whole country. Thousands were killed after the uprising was crushed by the military.

## BODY COUNT

No reliable figures are available, but estimates range between 3,000 and 10,000 killed in the "Rangoon Spring" uprising, and tens of thousand of people who opposed the regime have been killed since Ne Win came to power.

## FAMOUS QUOTES

"There is no need to stay in power when I have real power—the army."

"Soldiers are trained to shoot straight on order ... Let those inclined to anarchy be duly warned: If they have to face the troops it will be no laughing matter."